Driving the Uberverse

Diary of an Uber Driver
And Why I Switched to Lyft

Raymond A. Nadolny, Ph.D.

Driving the Uberverse
Diary of an Uber Driver
And Why I Switched to Lyft

Copyright 2018 Raymond A. Nadolny, Ph.D.

ISBN: 978-1-9867-9187-8
(also available for Kindle)

Book design and layout: Lighthouse24

CONTENTS

INTRODUCTION 1

PART ONE: UBER 5

    Chapter One: Getting the Job, No Skills Required 7

    Chapter Two: Novice Driver 13

    Chapter Three: UBER Driver 23

    Chapter Four: Does It Pay? 39

    Chapter Five: Honeymoon Period 56

    Chapter Six: Doubts 63

    Chapter Seven: Tips 77

    Chapter Eight: Divorce 87

PART TWO: LYFT OFF 105

    Chapter Nine: Driver's Perspective 107

    Chapter Ten: Control, We Have a Problem 121

    Chapter Eleven: Deal with the Devil 133

    Chapter Twelve: Weekend Driving 144

    Chapter Thirteen: Regret 157

    Chapter Fourteen: My Hero 166

CONCLUSION 171

INTRODUCTION

"Uber, the world's largest taxi company, owns no vehicles. Facebook, the world's most popular media owner, creates no content. Alibaba, the most valuable retailer, has no inventory. And Airbnb, the world's largest accommodation provider, owns no real estate. Something interesting is happening."[1]

Tom Goodwin

THIRTY YEARS AS an executive, the last seven years as president, I was ready to take a step back and enjoy some well-earned time pursuing my childhood passion, writing. Three problems got in the way: I became lonely; I got bored, and; I struggled with no longer being the primary provider.

First, I had forgotten how lonely writing can be. I wasn't used to being alone. For over ten years, I had been the center of a college community. Later, sitting in front of a keyboard in a twentieth-floor high-rise, I was suffocating, and I needed to get back into the world.

Second, as I came to realize very quickly, I cannot sit for eight hours. Most days, if I spent three hours writing, it was an outstanding day. I never came close to eight hours. I didn't have the patience and I needed a diversion.

Lastly, and maybe more importantly, I was used to a paycheck coming in every two weeks. I felt guilty about my morning coffee at Starbucks and my taste for fine clothes at Nordstrom's, as my wife, Joyce, continued to work, supporting the family as the last professional standing. I might be "semi-retired", but I did not want to go on spousal welfare in order to continue to enjoy the nicer things in life.

---

[1] https://techcrunch.com/2015/03/03/in-the-age-of-disintermediation-the-battle-is-all-for-the-customer-interface/

David

Sensing I was not adjusting to my new role as house husband/writer, Joyce treated me to happy hour at the Westin Hotel in downtown Bellevue. As it was a Sunday afternoon, we found ourselves alone in the bar. Joyce, a social butterfly, began a conversation with the bartender, David, who lived in Seattle, but commuted to Bellevue for work. I was curious and asked David: "Why do you make such a long commute when there are so many jobs in Seattle?" His reply was quick.

"Simple," he said. "I am also an Uber driver. In the morning, on my way to work, I pick up passengers that want to travel from Seattle to Bellevue. When I end my shift in Bellevue, I Uber passengers from Bellevue to Seattle."

Joyce and I knew about Uber, having used it numerous times in our own travels. Founded in 2009, Uber holds title to the world's largest ride sharing service. Eighteen years later, Uber is more than just the name of a company. Uber is the word people use to explain how one gets from point A, to point B. *Slate Magazine* put it best in a recent headline: "Let's Uber, I'll call a Lyft."[2] So, whether it is Uber, Lyft, or any of the other growing number of rideshare companies, people, like David, now have the opportunity to be their own boss in the exciting new world of rideshare.

I loved David, a sort of middle-aged, twenty-first century gypsy. Here was a guy with great people skills, leveraging dollars in the new gig economy. Sure, 85% of Gig workers make less than $500 per month,[3] but for people like David, there are additional cost savings, like free transportation to and from work, that no one was accounting. Not only was David carpooling, but David was both saving money and making money as a driver.

I, like many people, fantasized about doing Uber, but never seriously. David, over two cocktails, opened the door to a new world

---

[2] http://www.slate.com/articles/technology/technology/2017/12/why_people_who_stopped_using_uber_are_still_using_it_as_a_verb.html

[3] https://www.forbes.com/sites/sleasca/2017/07/17/highest-paying-jobs-gig-economy-lyft-taskrabbit-airbnb/#3f8ac03e7b64

for me. The world of rideshare was the answer, and Uber was a way out of my writing funk, my spending dilemma, and my waning self-esteem.

As a college president, I was constantly meeting new and interesting people and I could make a small difference or a big difference in people's lives, but it carried a sometimes overwhelming amount of responsibility. As an Uber driver, I thought, I could meet interesting people, perform a service, and maybe even make a small difference in the life of my passengers, but this time, with little responsibility. David became my new role model. I wanted to experience life as an urban gypsy.

Making a Commitment

I knew from the start that I did not want to be a driver whose sole mission was to get the passenger from point A to point B. I wanted passengers to feel like they were being cared for in an extraordinary way through the simplest of actions; carrying luggage, opening and closing the door, getting them to their destination or a meeting with plenty of time to spare. If a passenger wanted to stop for coffee, I would take them to the nearest Starbucks. And if they just needed someone to listen, I would offer them my full attention.

The class of car is important. My car, a fully equipped dark blue Chrysler 300, was several years old, but in excellent condition. The sophisticated interior provided a roomy experience, making for a luxurious ride. I would make it a point to keep the vehicle clean and vacuum the floors daily.

As I worked 10 years as a vice president and later, 7 years as a president, I knew how stressful life and work could become. My goal was to alleviate stress for the passenger in any way possible. If people asked me to wait ten minutes, I would do it with a smile, and believe me, smiling was not always easy.

As an executive, I knew I did not smile enough. So, while driving for Uber, I reminded myself repeatedly to smile when I greeted the passenger, when I opened the door for the passenger, or even when I looked at the passenger from my rear-view mirror. It was not enough to drive people in a luxurious car, I wanted the passenger's experience to be both warm and comforting.

So, I made a commitment to drive for three months. Three months would provide a good outlet and three months would provide opportunity to explore and document this exciting new world of rideshare. If I journaled my experiences religiously, I just might be able to provide a glimpse into this strange new world.

By the end of my first month, I knew I had the makings of a book. Stories and experiences came quicker than I could ever have imagined. I remember thinking, I have enough content for half a book. By the end of the second month, I was doubly amazed. I had enough material for a book.

My experience of driving has been life-changing: I found another calling; I got out of the house, meeting new and interesting people; and I found a modest income to support my discretionary needs. Making the change from president of a college to driver, I went from constantly "running around," to driving people constantly "running around." I might have been sitting in the front seat, but I always felt like a backseat spectator. Most of my passengers did not know it, but I was their greatest fan.

The Uberverse, as I began to call the world of rideshare, was a much larger world than I initially thought. But over time, I was fortunate to navigate my way around and learn the answer to many of the questions I entertained about this strange, new world: What is it like to be a driver? How do you become a driver? What are the passengers like? Do drivers make a livable wage? What is the difference between Uber and Lyft? Is it safe?

On reflection, I can honestly say that my driving experience has been one of the most enjoyable experiences of my career. As I am not quite ready to stop, I continue to be rewarded by the diverse and extraordinary individuals that step into my car. Who would have thought? Not only is driving an exciting experience for anyone looking for an adventure, but in an increasingly stressed-out country, I would find a little peace and a lot of hope as a rideshare driver.

Part One
UBER

CHAPTER ONE

GETTING THE JOB, NO SKILLS REQUIRED

Raymond Nadolny, Uber Driver
October 16, 2017, Monday

    Becoming an Uber driver is incredibly simple, maybe too simple. It could be the reason why so many have complained about Uber's vetting process for drivers, or more precisely, the lack of one. When I downloaded the Uber Driver app, Uber asked for permission to perform a criminal records check, which I consented. For a company that does not conduct one on one interviews, the lack of fingerprinting or a deep background check is concerning.

    I also had to take a short quiz on my knowledge of the Seattle area. I took the ten-question test, thinking a tourist could pass it. If there was a knowledge test for the job, this test was the extent of it. Anyone that can surf the web can pass this test, and that includes my eight-year old daughter, Emma, and my ten-year old daughter, Julia.

    I needed to complete four final tasks before I could become a driver. The first task was easy. I downloaded a picture of my Washington State Driver's license. As I just moved back to Washington State from North Dakota, I had not yet changed over my insurance and vehicle registration from North Dakota to Washington state. Once that was completed, I only needed to set up a time to get my car inspected.

    My goal was to get everything done in one day. Early Monday morning, I went to the DMV and had my plates changed from North Dakota to Washington. In less than an hour, I was in and out of the DMV, having replaced my North Dakota plates with brand new Washington State plates (Cost: $448.25, Ouch!)

The Uber Hub, A Strip Club and an Abandoned Parking Lot

Anyone in the Seattle area that wants to drive for Uber needs to pass a vehicle inspection at the Uber Greenlight Hub or Spot. The inspection was free and advertised to take less than 30 minutes. Uber, I knew, had four vehicle requirements: 1. Model year 2007 or newer; 2. 4-door car or minivan; 3. Good condition with no cosmetic damage and; 4. No commercial branding. I was good to go on all four requirements.

Looking at a map, the location of the Seattle Hub was only five hundred feet south of Safeco Field, home of the Seattle Mariners. I was getting excited, so while driving over, I multi-tasked and called State Farm to change over my insurance from North Dakota to Washington. State Farm assured me it would take only a couple of hours, and they would email me an ecard as proof of my Washington insurance.

I was quickly approaching the finish line. Not only was it possible to complete all of the requirements by early afternoon, but who knows, I thought, maybe I would take my first drive that very day. I could not wait for my maiden voyage and become a member of a company serving six hundred and thirty-three cities worldwide.

Entering Seattle, my anticipation building, I started to fantasize about driving into a palatial Uber Hub. There was no doubt about it, I was officially excited. On entering First Avenue, I took it as a personal challenge to arrive at my destination, 1714 First Avenue S, as if I was taking a passenger and their life depended on it. I failed. I passed the Uber Hub twice. Most likely, my virtual passenger would have died.

I passed the Uber Hub the first time as there were no signs in what ended up being a large, empty parking lot with a trailer set at the very back, adjacent to a barbwire fence, reminiscent of a concentration camp. The Hub was actually in one of Seattle's more seedy neighborhoods. The marquee building on the street was *Dream Girls at SoDo*, a strip club. The strip club was four hundred feet south of Safeco Field and the Hub was another hundred feet south of the strip club. Compared to the Uber Hub, the strip club looked like a palace.

I drove around the block, passed the strip club for a second time as there was no signage at the Uber Hub, and came to the conclusion that the deserted parking lot had to be the Hub. I pulled my car into what resembled a dodgy back alley chop-shop operation. For a company valued at seventy billion dollars, I was, shall I say, surprised.

I arrived ten minutes early for my noon appointment, as was my custom, not knowing that the hub did not actually open until noon. A young man was just putting up Uber signs on the chain-linked fence. I tried to make eye contact with him, but he was having none of it, making sure he was always looking away from me.

Okay, I thought. I arrived early. My fault. I will wait.

Over the next ten minutes, cars began to drive in and park. A small crowd began to form. My car stood out in a sea of older model vehicles. I stood out in both my age (older) and my color (white). I was feeling a little self-conscious.

A woman, who looked like she just graduated from college, walked on site. She took out some keys from her pocket and opened a door to what looked like an abandoned trailer. Once she got in, she opened the window and announced to the small crowd, "Uber is now open for car inspections."

An increasing number of drivers continued to arrive. As I arrived early, typical for a baby boomer, I was the first in line. I looked around and confirmed that not only was I the only white person, I was probably the only person over fifty. Jennifer, the Uber attendant, pointed at me and waived me forward.

From the look of things, it apparently did not matter that my appointment was for 12 pm. So I walked up to the trailer and said, "Good afternoon. Here is my car registration, and if it is okay, I will input my insurance card online later today. Other than the vehicle inspection, I believe that covers everything."

Jennifer picked up my registration, entered something into her computer, looked up and, with a big smile said, "Congratulations, once you pass the car inspection, all you need to do is download your insurance card, and you are all set to drive."

Positive affirmation. I loved it. Who cared if I was standing in an Uber sweat shop? I said, "Thank you! How long does the car inspection take?"

"Well," she said, "since you are the first person, it should only take a couple of minutes. If you wait by your car, Tony will come over and let you know the results."[4]

Seeing that the line was growing and not wanting to take any more of her time, I said, "Thank you."

I turned around, and walked back to my car. Tony, whom Uber calls an "Uber Expert", was already standing by my car. He walked around my car, looked under my car, and then drove it once around the parking lot. It couldn't have been more than five minutes when the Uber Expert walked up to me and said rather curtly, "Your vehicle has passed. I will upload the form to your account. You are free to go."

The final verdict from the "Uber Expert" might have been short and sweet, but I have to admit, no matter what the test, having someone tell you that you passed is always a good feeling. I got into my car, drove out of the parking lot, brimming with confidence, until I remembered that Jennifer forgot to return my vehicle registration. I called Jennifer on the phone and requested she mail it back to me. She said she would. She never did; another story for later.

State Farm, true to their word, emailed me my new insurance card. When I arrived home, I downloaded it on my phone and saw I was ready to take my first passengers. Fastest, easiest job I ever landed. Could it really be that easy? Given my Chicago upbringing, I thought there had to be a catch.

When I got home, I went online to see if there was any training required. I was stunned. No training required. On the other hand, I thought, trying to put a positive spin on my new employer, how difficult could it be to drive, something I had been doing for almost forty years?

---

[4] I did not realize it at the time, but there are actually several designations of Uber cars. My car was designated as UberX; a 4-door sedan in good condition; seats at least 4 passengers in addition to the driver; and working windows and air conditioning. The other car designations include UberXL (extra-large passenger cars) and UberSelect (mid-tier luxury cars). I am not sure why I didn't qualify for UberSelect but I didn't bother to ask as there was a long line of people now waiting behind me.

A little frustrated by my lack of finding any type of professional development online, I turned to the Uber app. The app is the driver's bible. It allows the driver to decide how, where, and when they pick up a passenger. Open the app and tap "Go Online" and the app will alert the driver for a passenger pick up. The app has a live map showing the location of the passenger, even providing step by step directions on how to get the passenger to their location. By providing banking details, you receive weekly payments. You even have the option of immediate payment at any time through the apps nifty dashboard.

I searched the Uber app and found a couple of tutorials. I breezed through them, mystified at the lack of content. I did take to heart Uber's admonition to keep the car clean. So tomorrow, I would get my car detailed. And maybe, just maybe, I would pick up my first passenger/s.[5]

Prepping the Car
October 17, 2017, Tuesday

Early Tuesday morning, eager for my new adventure, I brought my car to the shop to get it detailed. I was going full board on the car: inside detail and outside detail. Cost: $299. Wow, some pretty high startup costs to begin. The detail took five hours, but the detail work was worth it. The exterior glossy finish was restored to the car's original condition. On the inside, even the small upholstery stains were removed. My car, three years old, looked brand new.

While my car was being detailed, I went online to Amazon to buy some accessory items to make the passenger's experience more enjoyable. Given Seattle weather patterns, my first purchase was an umbrella. Seattleites have an inside joke that the only people that use an umbrella in Seattle are tourists. I anticipated that many of my passengers would be tourists needing protection from the rain.

---

[5] I decided I would record the various costs associated with driving. Today, I spent $448.25 to get my plates changed. I also drove 20 miles round trip to the Uber Hub for the review of my car. Let's chalk up the expense to a new suit for a job interview, although I am pretty sure I did not see a dress code anywhere, whether online, on the app, or at the Hub.

My big purchase was an iPhone dock. Joyce and the kids always scolded me when I used my iPhone while driving. The dock would charge my phone while allowing me to not to have to pick it up each time I needed to refer to the map.

Auto detail completed, accessory items on their way, I was good to go. My daughter, Julia, had gymnastics in the evening, so I thought I might get my first fare after I dropped her off. I was pumped. When my wife and Emma decided to watch Julia at practice, I nixed driving as gymnastic's practice had turned into a family event. I wasn't greatly disappointed. Part of me was a little anxious. I wasn't sure what the experience would be like. Was I expecting too much?

I realized I was becoming just as anxious about driving for Uber as my first day working in higher education. Having achieved a lifetime of successes, a lingering doubt started to nag at me. Maybe I was not cut out for driving? Was I afraid of failing?

After a little soul-searching, I told myself that no matter what, I would make it work. And while I was being honest, I decided I might as well share with Joyce the startup costs as I was almost a grand in the hole before I even began. Joyce listened patiently and almost seemed envious of my new career. Since we were not reliant on the income and as Joyce was just as interested as I was in this new world of rideshare, she was surprisingly supportive, even suggesting I write a "Diary of an Uber Car Driver". That sealed the deal.

Joyce's confidence was all I needed to summon my courage to make my entrance in this strange new world. I was in the middle of writing a book on Irish folklore, but I would set it aside temporarily. Thousands of years of Irish folklore could wait a few months for this glance into 21st century innovation. I would begin a more formal diary around my experience with ridesharing versus the occasional scribblings. No more procrastinating; tomorrow would begin my new life.[6]

---

[6]*Today's Uber Startup Costs*: IPhone Dock and Umbrellas: $42.18. Interior and Exterior Detail: $300.

CHAPTER TWO

NOVICE DRIVER

Virgin Driver, A Rough Start
October 18, 2017, Wednesday

I had to bring my youngest girl, Emma, to the dentist and then drive her to school. It was perfect. After I delivered my daughter safely to school, I would turn on my Uber Driver app and launch into my first Uber drive. What better way to start my Uber experience?

As soon as I dropped off Emma, I nervously switched the app to the on position for the first time. I did not have to wait long as I was immediately hailed by Lisa, a ten-minute drive away. I was quickly off on my first journey.

Lisa lived just outside of Bellevue in a subdivision filled with large homes. She was waiting for me on the sidewalk, suitcase in hand. I pulled over to the curb, jumped out of the car, confirmed her name, picked up her suitcase and placed it in the trunk of my car. I didn't have a chance to open the door for her as she was inside my car before I could close my trunk. No matter, great start.

When I got back into the car, I pressed the button on the app confirming that I picked up Lisa. Nothing happened. Tap. Tap. Tap… Still nothing. I looked all over for some button to hit to get the fare started. Tap. Tap. Tap… Aghhhhhhh!

A bit self-consciously, but with a straight face, I turned to Lisa and said; "Were you able to start the trip on your app? Mine is not responding."

Lisa fumbled for a moment with her phone, and then she said, "No, mine is also not working."

Both of us tried for a minute longer to no avail. Frustrated, I made a decision. Lisa was the customer. I did not want her to be late to the airport, so I said: "Look, my first priority is to get you to your destination – the airport. I am going to get you to the airport. I will call Uber later to correct whatever technical difficulty existed."

Lisa, like all people worried about making their flight, looked relieved, but not completely settled. I am sure she was wondering whether she would be charged the rate Uber identified when she requested the ride, or if she would be taken for a ride by a total stranger. I attempted to reassure her, "When I call Uber, I will make sure the charge is exactly for what was identified to you. I will also make a complaint."

That seemed to settle Lisa down and without my asking, she started to tell me about her travel plans. "I am flying Southwest Airlines to attend my brother's wedding in Annapolis, Maryland."

"That sounds like a fun trip," I said.

"Not really. It is my brother's third marriage."

The conversation was starting to get interesting. Lisa was also attractive and I wanted to ask why she was travelling on her own. I knew she wanted to talk to me, but I found myself, well, shy?

I did not realize how quickly a conversation with a complete stranger could become so personal, even intimate. I was not quite ready to hear the details of her brother's third marriage. Plus, I was green and I did not want to look too green.

I decided to change the conversation: "Lisa, what is the best way out of your neighborhood?"

Lisa obliged and directed me to the highway. By the time we were on the highway, we were only a short hop, skip and a jump from the airport. As we arrived, I pulled over to the curb, jumped out of the car, grabbed her suitcase, and opened the door for her. She stepped out of the car with a big smile on her face, thanked me, took her suitcase, turned and walked away. It wasn't a clean drive, but all the same, I competed my first drive.

My first task was to correct my problem with the app. How could I even accept another ride if I couldn't even operate the app. I drove a little further, pulled my car over and checked the app to see if I could identify an Uber helpline. If there was a number, it was difficult to find. And... I could see that the app was still expecting me to pick up Lisa. I was getting frustrated.

After some playing around on the app, I realized the problem. I was trying to tap a button when the action required was a simple swipe of the button. Nothing was mentioned about a swipe in the tutorials. Why didn't anyone say that? Still, I felt like an idiot.

Once I made the swipe, Lisa's ride began, now providing me the route from my current location at the airport to her house, and then back to the airport. I tried to end the ride, but Uber would not let me. Now what do I do?

I drove another couple of miles and pulled over once again. I made my second swipe and was able to finally end the ride. According to the app, my earnings for the ride was two dollars and seventy-one cents. Lisa's bill would be a little over four dollars. She would undoubtedly be pleased. While I drove thirty minutes back home in traffic, I realized I basically provided Lisa a free ride, or should I say, a ride at my loss.

Surprisingly, I was not angry. I chalked up the ride and the loss as a learning experience. At the very least, I was now familiar with how the app worked. Plus, I was still pretty excited that I actually accomplished my first ride in spite of my rookie error. And I liked Lisa. Eager to please, I may not have been ready to listen, but I knew in the future, I would be more prepared for personal disclosures by the passengers.

Plus, while searching for how to turn the app on, I came across an option to include personal information about myself. Maybe the personal information was used to increase conversation between the passenger and driver or maybe it was a way of obtaining tips. I didn't know. But as I enjoyed my experience with Lisa, I would seriously think about entering some personal information. I called it a day and returned home. There was a lot to take in and a lot to write.

Five Stars

October 19, 2017, Thursday

Passengers can rate drivers on a scale of one star to five stars, five stars being the highest. I woke up in the morning and immediately checked my app to check to see if Lisa left a rating. The rating showed five stars. I was elated. I made my first trip, made some decisions that resulted in a financial loss, but at the same time, fulfilled my obligation to the customer. I was rewarded with five stars and it felt great.

It is probably important to disclose that a five-star rating, even though it is Uber's highest rating, is fairly common. If a driver's average rating drops below 4.6 stars, he or she can be deactivated. I have listened to many drivers complain about having a 4.95 rating.

I was a little puzzled at the lack of the tip, but I heard that for the longest time, the tipping option was not available on Uber. So, I chalked up the absence of tips as passengers used to not tipping. What I did not know was that while the tipping option was added during Uber's "180 Days of Change", the tipping option had not yet been introduced to the Seattle market. Poor communication from Uber. So, for my first three weeks, I just believed people did not want to tip.

As I was operating under the false delusion I could receive tips, I decided to enter one piece of personal information about myself in the app and see if that might encourage a customer to tip. I disclosed that I grew up in Chicago. At the very least, it might start a conversation from passengers with connections to Chicago.

Later, during the day, I had second thoughts on offering such a small piece of information. Maybe, I thought, I should have shared that I have four daughters, a stepdaughter in college, a stepdaughter entering college, and the two youngest daughters still at home. I decided to wait and give it a little more thought before I entered any information about myself. I needed to be more cautious. Did I really know who was going to step into my vehicle? I needed to know more about my passengers before I disclosed anything too personal about myself and my family.

Ferdinand

Early in the morning, I dropped the kids at their bus stop and turned on my Uber app anticipating my next Uber adventure. A call came in and off I went.

Driving to the W, an upscale hotel in downtown Bellevue, I passed Ferdinand, standing amidst a throng of other people waiting for rides, as he was busily staring into his phone. I turned around and drove back slowly to the small group of people waiting for rides, when Ferdinand flagged me down.

Ferdinand, a consultant in his late 20s, stepped into my car and immediately apologized. This time, I prepared myself in advance to listen, but as Ferdinand was knee-deep in business, I thought the trip would be quiet. I was wrong.

When I heard Ferdinand's accent, I asked, "Where are you from?"

"I was born and raised in Berlin, Germany," he said. "Right now, I live in San Francisco."

That intrigued me. I asked Ferdinand, "What do you do for a living?"

"When I was in Germany, I earned my graduate degree in mechanical engineering. I now provide consulting to Microsoft engineers on management strategies. So, every week for the last six months, I've been flying from San Francisco, where I now live, to Seattle."

"That's a lot of travel," I said.

"I know," Ferdinand said with a groan. "I have to tell you, I love this area. I am trying to convince my girlfriend to make the move to Bellevue."

"That's a pretty big move. Has she been here?"

"She visited a few weeks ago, and she loved Bainbridge Island, so I am hopeful on a possible move to the pacific northwest."

The commute from Bainbridge Island to Microsoft was a minimum one and a half hour ride each way, requiring car travel and a trip on the state's ferry system. I asked Ferdinand, "Are you ready to undertake such a long commute?"

Without hesitation, Ferdinand said, "Absolutely."

I didn't say it, but, wow, Ferdinand was in love. It felt good seeing a young man in love.

Ferdinand asked, "Do you have any family?"

"Yes," I answered. "I am married. My wife is senior corporate counsel for SAP, here in Bellevue. I have two daughters and two stepdaughters with our oldest attending the University of Washington."

Ferdinand nodded in appreciation and then started expounding on the benefits of attending a university in Germany. The universities were free. We talked about my trip to Germany over the summer and then went into a deeper discussion on eastern Germany's economy, ending our conversation covering inflation on the west coast, a four-hundred percent increase in a tech stock he invested in, local housing prices and more. I was surprised at the number of topics covered. It was a little bit like a ping pong match with both of us lobbing over insights.

The ride was a little more than twenty minutes, and in that short time, we managed to bond. I dropped off Ferdinand, feeling very satisfied. It was exactly what I hoped for. No, it was more than I hoped for. For a short period of time, I was not only able to enter into another person's world, but I was able to enjoy it. I made a couple of dollars, I learned something new, and I made a connection.

Maybe being an Uber driver in Bellevue/Redmond/Seattle area was much different than other areas because of the high number of white collar workers in the area. This was only my second ride, so could I really expect similar experiences day after day? No matter, Ferdinand made my day.

I had much to write about and needed to get home to accurately document our conversation. I did not want to betray my passenger's trust, so I made the decision in advance not to record my conversations. Given everything we discussed, I was slightly regretting that decision.

As I was driving home, I looked down to check how much I made on the ride: thirty dollars and ninety-two cents for a 6.7-mile drive that took 21.27 minutes to complete. Ka-ching! What a change from yesterday.

The app had the fares broken down neatly.

Base Fare	$ 1.01
Distance	$ 6.79
Time	$ 3.82
Surge	$18.60

I immediately caught sight of the reason for my jackpot earnings. During busy times like rush hour and when the number of riders exceed the number of drivers, Uber increases its fares by adding a surge charge. I was driving in the rain in the middle of morning rush hour, hence an additional surge charge of eighteen dollars and sixty cents.

The jackpot earnings made me have second thoughts about calling it a day and returning home. Nah, I was delighted and continued on my way home. I was riding on cloud nine and did not want to ruin the moment, given the large number of personalities that could step into my car next.

Stood Up
October 20, 2017, Friday

I had two housekeeping items to take care of before I picked up my first passenger of the day. First, I installed the iPhone dock. The dock certainly allowed me to drive with more confidence, knowing that I can talk on the phone and view directions while keeping my hands on the wheel. Second, the umbrella arrived a day earlier, so I placed it on the passenger seat for easy access. I then dropped off my daughters at school and turned on the Uber app… Silence.

As I drove home, the Uber app on, no one signaled me for a ride. Wow, 8:30 am on a Friday morning. I felt a little dejected. Hmmmm. So, I pulled into my parking garage and went back up to my condo. There was no way I could keep the app on in my condo and expect to get to my car in a timely manner to respond to a passenger call from the twentieth floor. I should have brought a book as it would have given me a reason to wait a little longer in the car. No matter, I would try again on Monday. My first week as an Uber driver exceeded my expectations. I was not going to rush the experience.

Too Close to Home
October 23, 2017, Monday

After a long weekend, I could not wait to drop off the girls at their bus stop so I could return to my Uber trek. Once I performed my parental duties, and to my immediate delight, a ride was requested. To my shock, the pick-up location for my third ride ever, was at the high-rise where I was living. It never occurred to me I would eventually pick up someone from my building.

My family lives on the 20th floor of Bellevue Pacific Tower, a luxury condo building with amazing views and many amenities which include a 24-hour concierge, an exercise room, a pool/hot tub, and a rooftop garden. The people I know in the building are attorneys, business owners, and a large number of IT professionals. I did not know of anyone driving for Uber.

My pride got the best of me and I could tell I was embarrassed. It was hard to admit, but I was not ready for anyone in the high-rise to know I was driving for Uber. Besides my wife, I had not told another soul.

Was I too close to my last position as president of a college and felt my Uber work was somehow beneath me? What is wrong making a little extra money on the side? I am pretty sure the first question more accurately reflected my situation. I chalked my feelings up to arrogance, vanity, and pride, bit the bullet, and I returned home to pick up my passenger.

Then I thought, on the other hand, maybe I won't know the person. Maybe I can slip in and out with no one knowing what I was am doing.

Lucas' Father

I drove up to the entrance and met Lucas and his father, Edward, at the front door. Scanning the circular drive, I was in luck; we were alone. Lucas, a 27-year old Microsoft employee from Brazil, whom I never met before, was waiting for me. The man I would be driving was Lucas' 79-year-old father, Edward, a retired engineer who was visiting.

I picked up Edward's two large bags, placed them into the trunk of my car, and off we went. As I was driving out, I looked around once more to see if anyone else had entered into the circular drive. My secret was safe, and I breathed a sigh of relief.

I could not help but think I was being a total fool. Fortunately, for my vain self, I had bigger fish to fry than my personality deficiencies. I was still having a difficult time using the Uber app.

For my first three rides, I had trouble navigating to the destinations. I realized for the first time that when I picked up a passenger and made my initial swipe, navigation did not immediately start. Instead, when I confirmed the rider with one swipe, I discovered I had to do a second swipe to set the navigation in motion. Swiping the navigation button, I was greeted by the courteous sound of Uber's Alexa, the voice guided navigation system, directing me to the destination. Great, I thought, this is getting easier.

Edward was both friendly and chatty. As he was retired, he planned the trip three weeks before his arrival. Edward was from Sao Paolo, Brazil and was headed to the airport to take a Delta flight to Chicago. The trip to Chicago was a side trip for pleasure prior to his return to Brazil as he had never been to Chicago. As I was born and raised in Chicago, we made a pretty quick connection.

Over the course of the ride, Edward talked about his son living alone, his son's place being a bit messy, and his other son who was currently going to school at the University of Sao Paolo (also studying engineering). I was delighted, listening to the proud father talking about his sons, and asked the occasional question so that he knew I was interested.

Edward, a retired engineer, shared with me, "I still feel young at 69. You know, my son has a brand new black Mustang which I was able to drive."

Edward's excitement was contagious. I wondered if his son knew how proud his dad was of him. As I made my way through thick traffic, I was still smiling as I squeezed in between two parked cars and double-parked at Delta arrival.

Edward continued talking. The traffic was bumper-to-bumper. I needed to get Edward's two bags out of the car and move my car before security paid me a visit, but I did not want to cut Edward off. So, I opened my door, left it partly open, in an attempt to both listen to Edward and retrieve his bags out of my trunk.

When Edward stepped out of the car, I looked him in the eyes, shook his hand and wished him a great time in Chicago. He responded with a broad smile. My father passed away six months earlier and I became sentimental. I wanted to remind him to tell his son how proud he was of him. I almost gave him a hug goodbye until I remembered that I was an Uber driver and not a family friend.

I was immensely pleased with myself on the way back, which was good because the return traffic was heavy. I also had time to review what I earned from the trip. Edward's son paid forty-one dollars and sixty-five cents for his father's ride. I made twenty-two dollars and fifty cents for the round trip, fifty-minute drive. Uber's share was seventeen dollars and five cents for the trip, which made me think Uber was making way too much money. I would learn later that Uber had been losing billions.

The return from the airport was also costing me money. Passengers cannot be picked up at the arrival gates. The airport designated a drop point for Uber drivers to pick up fares. I had no idea of the location of the drop point. I wasn't even sure if I would be allowed in the drop point (I had heard there might be some additional restrictions). Later, I thought, I would identify the location of the drop point and find out for sure about the restrictions

When I got close to Bellevue, I turned the app back on, but no fares were requested, so I returned home. I thought, $22.50 was worth it just for the pleasure of meeting and getting to know Edward. Anyway, my wife is going to lunch and would probably spend $20 for her meal.

As I was just getting started, I used $20 as my goal for the day. Goal accomplished. And, maybe, just maybe, I made a couple of people happy.

CHAPTER THREE

UBER DRIVER

Arjun

October 24, 2017, Tuesday

After three rides, I could now say I was completely confident in my ability to pick up a passenger and bring them to their destination. So, my goal for today was to complete two rides. Out of the gate, I was tagged by Arjun, who was staying at the downtown Sheraton. Being familiar with the Bellevue area has its perks, as I arrived quickly.

Arjun and I hit it off immediately. Arjun earned his masters and Ph.D. at Georgia Tech. A native of India, Arjun was proud of his alma mater. Georgia Tech ranked number five for engineering schools.

Arjun worked for Amazon and I was driving him to the Amazon office in Seattle. It was my first Uber fare both to Seattle and Amazon's Seattle Campus. I had never been to the Amazon campus, and was looking forward to my first trip.

I asked Arjun, "How do you like it in the United States?"

"Actually, I have been thinking about moving back to India."

"Why?" I said, a little astonished.

"I make a good living in the United States, but the cost of living is so high. I am not sure if living here is worth it. But because of the tech industry, India has become dirty. So, I am not sure if I want to go back."

I could tell that Arjun was truly conflicted about whether to stay in the United States or return to India. He continued, "The biggest challenge is with my family. I am married. Although my six brothers and sisters live in India, my wife's family have all moved from India to the United States. And now, we are trying to have our first child."

I thought the chances of Arjun moving back were small. On the other hand, could Arjun even survive at Amazon? Amazon may be one of the country's most esteemed businesses, but in the Seattle area, it has a reputation for being a brutal workplace. I heard employees talking about long hours. Arjun's story was consistent with what I heard.

I asked, "Do you enjoy your work at Amazon?"

Arjun said, "I previously worked at Bell Labs and have only recently come over to Amazon. I am starting to wonder whether I can really work for anyone as I am having some serious problems at work."

"I have heard Amazon is a tough place to work."

Arjun then opened up about his struggles, "It feels like a dog eat dog environment. It wouldn't be so bad if it was just a supervisor you did not get along with. You know that's just the business world and you just deal with it. At Amazon, it is doubly bad. If you end up with a supervisor you do not like, you are also trying to deal with that supervisor in an oppressive corporate culture."

I told Arjun about the corporate culture of my wife's workplace at SAP, a company he also heard about. *Fortune* just ranked SAP as one of the best 100 companies to work. Headquartered in Germany, employees felt like they belonged to a global community. Apparently, that feeling did not translate over to Amazon.

At some point, I felt like we were speed-talking as a steady stream of information and experiences were passed back and forth. Arjun was a good communicator and he was incredibly talented. Arjun was also an inventor.

Arjun told me, "I have 45 patents to my name."

"That's incredible!"

"But I no longer believe in patents. Ideas need to be free. I am disappointed that my education at Georgia Tech didn't include starting a business before I graduated. I do not understand why American colleges do not include this experience."

I didn't know how to respond. I loved listening to Arjun talk and the number of viewpoints he expressed in a short period of time.

Instead, I said, "You have such a warm way of speaking with people. You are able to express ideas that may be different from my own, but you do so in an informative way."

Arjun seemed delighted, so the timing was excellent. We were just pulling up to his building on the Amazon campus. I pulled over and then reached back to shake Arjun's hand. I wanted to tell him, "I have every confidence in you. Whether you stay in the United States or move back to India, you will be successful. Your family is fortunate to have you." But as an Uber driver, I might be operating a confessional, but I wasn't sure what degree of cheerleading was appropriate or just creepy.

I needed to find a place to stop and write up my conversation with Arjun. But Seattle traffic was crazy, so I decided to return. When I got back onto Bellevue Way, I thought, as I hadn't reached my goal and I was feeling pumped up by my conversation with Arjun, what the heck, I'd do a second fare.

Incredibly, the next fare was at the AC Park Hotel, across the street from where I lived. Wow, two fares in one day to Seattle. I had an additional perk. The Uber route to the passenger's destination would take me close to Bill Gate's house which I never saw (spoiler alert, you can't see it from the street). Double bonus. It was an unusually sunny day and I was having the time of my life, enjoying magnificent views of the Olympic Mountains, Cascade Mountains, and Mount Rainier.

Mike

Mike stepped into the car and immediately started to prep a presentation he was about to make at the University of Washington Innovation Lab. While Mike worked, I was able to enjoy beautiful views of Lake Washington and Seattle while reflecting on my conversation with Arjun.

When we got onto 520, a floating bridge, Mike lifted his head, looked at the backdrop of the Olympic mountains behind Seattle and said, "Beautiful day today."

"It sure is," I acknowledged. "We only get 150 days of sun a year, so days like this are pretty special. Are you familiar with the area?"

"Yes. I own two businesses. One is in North Carolina and the other is close to the University of Washington," he said.

"Pretty impressive, businesses on opposite coasts," I said. "My stepdaughter is a senior at the University of Washington. She is currently on a study abroad program in China."

Mike left his presentation for a few moments to say proudly, "My daughter is a college senior in North Carolina. She's also on a study abroad program, but in Sidney, Australia."

We bonded, two fathers talking about the tremendous opportunities for our daughters and, as a bonus, the low costs associated with each of the programs. When we got to the UW Innovation Lab, I dropped Mike off and waited to see if he would reach over to shake my hand. He did.

I found parking and walked into the University of Washington Innovation Lab. I decided to write up my experience in one of their many lounges. I went through the Uber Driver app and saw that I spent one hour and nineteen minutes on the road, making thirty-seven dollars and eight cents. I spent seven dollars and seventy cents in tolls so my total earnings was thirty dollars and ten cents. Given mileage and expenses on the car, I wondered whether Uber drivers made a decent living, especially in the Seattle area. I needed to speak with Joyce, who was a master at excel spreadsheets. I needed to break down the costs to see what I was actually earning.

As I began to write up the day, I realized that even on short trips, a great deal of information was being passed back and forth between the passenger and me. Oftentimes, I had a hard time remembering the name of the passenger, much less spelling the name. There had to be another way of capturing the narrative from my rides.

I decided to purchase a digital recorder. I would not record the conversations, but at least between rides, I could record some of the more important moments. The irony did not escape me when I quickly purchased a digital recorder on Amazon.

All in all, the day was fantastic. Even on my way home, autumn was working its magic as I drove by trees covered with bright red and dark orange leaves. I thought, the conversation with both men was worth the drive alone. In fact, I would have driven Arjun for free.

FIVE STAR RATING
October 26, 2017, Thursday

Rohan

After dropping my daughters off to school, I picked up my first fare at the W, a luxury hotel owned by the Marriott in downtown Bellevue. Like Ferdinand, a couple of days earlier, I passed Rohan as he was buried in his phone. On my second pass at the W, Rohan flagged me down.

Rohan, of Indian descent, was another consultant commuting from San Jose to Bellevue. So far, the number of males from San Jose of Indian descent flying out on a weekly basis from San Jose, California, was startling. Rohan's destination was T-Mobile in Factoria, just south of Bellevue. I didn't even know that T-Mobile had a campus in the Bellevue area, so I looked forward to the trip.

Rohan spent the entire trip on his phone. As a consultant for T-Mobile, at least in my mind, he remained true to his work, making the most of his time in the car. After some initial traffic, I made great time to the T-Mobile campus. Bellevue's T-Mobile location was much larger than I realized with two large buildings and pretty decent security. I was waved into a designated area for drop-offs. Even as Rohan stepped out of the car, he managed not to trip, even though his face was still pressed to his phone.

Driving off the T-Mobile campus, I thought, the number of businesses in the Seattle area is truly impressive. Maybe every senior in high school should do an Uber stint. What a great way for young people not only get to know the area, but get an appreciation of the diversity of businesses in the community. And if one got lucky, they could get some insight from the passengers on the various careers.

I went online later that day to find out the minimum age to drive for Uber. I was disappointed to see it was twenty-one. So much for my high school idea.

Looking down on my app, I saw I earned eight dollars and forty-one cents on the trip. Disappointing. This was my lowest earnings for a drive to date. But then again, I was only on the road for 16 minutes and

36 seconds. Uber made three dollars and forty-nine cents so I felt a little better about my paltry earnings.

I needed to get a better idea on my real earnings. I talked to Joyce, the spreadsheet master, the night before and she committed to putting together a spreadsheet for me. So at least for next week, I would do a better job at seeing and understanding my real earnings.

I was thinking of going home when I decided to look at my ratings. I had a total of 3 five star ratings (up from one just a day earlier) and, more notably, a compliment. The compliment was my first. I swiped the compliment button and saw "Great conversation," most probably from Arjun. I was totally pumped. Not everyone was going to provide a rating, but when they did, and if it was positive, it was certainly an adrenaline rush. I was soon off to get my next fare.

Mark

I picked up Mark in front of his house, which happened to be close to my daughter's grade school. Mark was going to Seattle and although friendly, he was not talkative so the trip was quiet. Instead of taking the 520, the app took me across I-90 (Seattle's second floating bridge) which meant no tolls. I liked that. Plus, I enjoyed another opportunity to take in Seattle's skyline.

When I got near Safeco Field, Mark asked me to drop him off at a nearby Shell gas station which I did. I was thinking of parking somewhere and writing up my day's reflections, but Seattle's south side can be a little seedy with a high population of transients. I saw one homeless man yelling into his cellphone, then beating his chest with his cell phone, and then acting like he was going to throw his cell phone across the street. My guess was mental illness. Some of the homeless were pushing grocery carts piled with what looked like their world belongings, others looked fatigued, ravaged by time. In a world many do not see, I thought, this place, these people, deserve their own story.

Once I got to Rainier Street, I hopped back on I-90 and was quickly home. Total earnings for the day: twenty-one dollars and sixty-three cents. Total earnings for the week so far: eighty-one dollars and ninety-three cents. After tomorrow, I had no doubt I would meet my goal of earning one hundred dollars for the week. Sure, it was not a lot of money, given the time I put into driving. But I was really enjoying the experience.

HALLOWEEN WEEKEND
October 27, 2017, Friday

I debated whether I should drive in the morning as became my custom, or drive in the evening to take advantage of Halloween weekend traffic. According to Uber, surge pricing would go into effect to accommodate the increase in traffic. But every time Uber offered surge pricing, I noticed it only applied to Seattle. I made the decision to follow my morning routine and accomplish my one hundred dollar goal in Bellevue. Plus, I heard stories of drivers having to deal with drunk passengers and I wanted a little more experience before taking on that headache.

John

I picked up my first passenger at the Silver Cloud Inn in Bellevue. John, wearing a Chicago Bears shirt, was returning to his home in Springfield, Illinois. We had an immediate connection due to our Chicago roots.

John was that typical Midwest all-American. "Been a tough few years to be a Chicago Bears fan," I said.

"Looks like this year will be painful," he said in empathetic misery.

"Are you from Chicago?"

"No, but I grew up in Wheaton, Illinois. My parents divorced when I was a child, so I lived in Wheaton with my dad during the summer and my mother the rest of the year in Springfield, Illinois."

"How did you get from Wheaton to Bellevue?" I asked.

"My wife and I actually rented a house in Northern Lynwood for a year, while I worked for an insurance company in Bellevue. The commute was difficult, so I asked my company if I could work remotely. I told them I was willing to take a reduction in pay. The company not only allowed me to work remotely, but they paid me the same rate. We sold our home in Wheaton, which we kept and had been renting, and I moved my family (wife, four-year old boy, and newborn son) from Lynwood, Washington to Springfield, Illinois where we now live on West Coast wages."

John said this all with a big smile. I could see the headline: "Midwest boy makes it big, but remains in the Midwest." Conventional, friendly, John personified both the values and the work ethic of the Midwest, and he was excited to be going home.

He told me, "My son is four years old, and is looking forward to Halloween. I am pretty excited about going home."

John was a pleasure to listen to as he possessed that "attitude of gratitude". He appreciated what life provided him. Whether the losing Bears, travelling to make his job work, his good fortune to make a decent wage and live in the Midwest, or his family, John had the unique ability to make one feel better by just being in his presence.

I wanted to hear more, but before I knew it, we arrived at the airport. I thought about asking him about his son's costumes, but I returned to my role as driver, got out, retrieved his bags, and opened his door. As John stepped out of the car, we wished each other a Happy Halloween. I would love to have been a fly on the wall when John gave the costume to his son.

Pulling away, I looked down at my app and saw that I reached my goal of hundred dollars. Reaching a goal, no matter the size, always feels good. And like all passengers like John, where I feel so much better about humankind, I decided I would take another passenger. Good fortune struck once again and his name was Lim.

Lim

Lim arrived the night before from Beijing. A tall man with a large and warm smile, I was immediately taken in by the charm of this gentle Chinese giant. I said: "You look great for a person who should be jet-lagged."

Lim nodded in agreement, "I work at the Microsoft Office in Beijing and will only be in town for a week so it is good. I am happy to be in Seattle, taking in the changing colors. I love fall and Seattle is especially beautiful now."

"International trips for short stays must be difficult."

"Yes, but I am going to be at meetings all day and they will be more difficult. I have a hard time keeping up with the English."

I complimented Lim on his English, praise which he immediately downplayed, so I asked him, "What percent of English can you follow when attending a meeting?"

"80 percent," he said.

"My wife speaks several languages," I told him. "We have friends from Japan and she becomes our translator. After a night of translating, she is mentally exhausted, so I can certainly understand."

Lim again nodded. "Have you ever been to China?" he asked.

"Yes, once. My oldest daughter is there right now in Beijing on a study abroad program."

Lim was delighted and started to ask me numerous questions. By the end of his questions, I felt like I could have asked Lim to hire Kiana as an intern or even have her stay with his family. But I reminded myself, I am an Uber driver, so I changed directions. "When I was in Beijing, the pollution was terrible. How is it now?"

"We are working on it," he said with a sigh.

We engaged in what seemed to be a lengthy conversation at the changing environment in Beijing. When I think about the conversation, it could not have been that long as the entire trip only took thirteen minutes, thirteen seconds. But with Lim, I felt lost in time.

As we arrived at the Microsoft campus, I pulled over, jumped out, ran around to the other side of the car, and opened the door for Lim. Lim thanked me, and then shook my hand. I was honored.

Once again, I was exceedingly happy with my day. I spent only one hour and eight minutes on the road while making thirty-one dollars and sixty-seven cents. The frosting on the cake – two fascinating stories of two people that truly appreciate life. Maybe I should have paid them? Today, I was the one appreciating life. I now earned one-hundred and thirteen dollars and sixty cents for the week.

Driving became a breath of fresh air, maybe even an addiction. I didn't want to stop, so why stop? And as I had never done three trips in a row, I decided to do one final trip.

Crystal

I went to 1st Street in downtown Bellevue, which was not a street, but actually an alley behind Bellevue's Main Street. Crystal was nowhere to be seen. Two women were walking down the street, so I presumed one of them was Crystal. I stared, they walked faster. Nope, not my passenger. I am sure I came across as a stalker.

I drove further down the alley and pulled up behind Glassybaby, an art store that featured hand-blown glass, but Crystal was nowhere to be found. I called her on the phone. "I am at the destination identified on my GPS. Are you ready?"

Crystal responded, "I am at the front of the store, on Main Street."

After two incredible rides, I could feel the letdown. Unless the passenger enters the address on the app, the app will most likely not transmit the actual destination if it only relies on GPS. In Crystal's case, she opened her Uber app in the store, closer to 1st Street, the alley at the back of the store. Crystal then walked through the store, out the front door, through the small parking lot, and waited for me on the sidewalk on Main Street. So, there we sat, me parked in the back of the store, and Crystal waiting for me at the front of the store.

I was explaining this to Crystal on the phone as I pulled up in front of Glassybaby. Crystal was standing on the sidewalk, her back to the street looking in the direction of the store, taking no notice that I was now behind her. Still talking on the phone, Crystal asked me where I wanted her to go, to which I replied, "My car is right next to you." She turned around, laughed and opened the car door to get in.

As Crystal made herself comfortable in the car, I identified on my app that I had picked up the passenger. Uber does not start paying when you are enroute to the pickup point. So wandering around, trying to find Crystal, came out of my pocket.

I turned my attention back to my passenger. "Shopping on Main Street?" I asked.

Crystal had met a friend to shop for hand-blown glass at Glassybaby. They were shopping for votive lights which start at fifty dollars. She said, "I bet you think that is a lot of money for a votive light."

"The Seattle area is known for its glass art, so it makes sense." I said. "I live two blocks from here, so I am actually a little embarrassed that I didn't even know of the existence of the store. I walk up and down this street at least once a week, so I must have passed it every time."

"There are three Glassybaby stores in the area," Crystal said proudly and then quickly changed the subject, "Do you also drive for Lyft? I know a lot of Uber drivers do."

"I don't drive for Lyft," I answered. "But I might consider it later."

Crystal knew quite a bit about Uber. "My husband and I were talking about Uber and were wondering how much a driver actually makes. If you take in wear and tear on the car, gas, etc., can a driver really make any money?"

I smiled at the bluntness of Crystal's question. "I have not been doing this for very long, but I am guessing between ten dollars to fifteen dollars an hour, obviously not a livable wage in the land of the $50 glass votive."

Crystal laughed. I shared with Crystal my limited driving experience. "Driving would be a good way for young people to get to know both the area and the many businesses we have in the Seattle area. It is too bad that the minimum age is 21, since I originally thought it would be a great job for seniors in high school, but that is not going to work."

Crystal had an idea. "I think college students should really explore the opportunity."

"That's a great idea," I said. "Unfortunately, the driver's car insurance has to be in the driver's name. I imagine most college students still have their car insurance in their parent's name."

We made a collective sigh just as I pulled in front of Crystal's beautiful Issaquah home. I waited for her to go inside, wondering why a woman with a two-car garage would be taking an Uber. She turned around and saw me waiting. As a young man, I was always taught to wait until the woman was safely inside. Probably not the thing to do as a driver. Uber is a different culture and I am sure, although my heart was in the right place, I only left a creepy impression. I will most likely drive off next time.

THE BEACH
October 28, 2017, Saturday

Tonight, I decided to do my first evening drive. First, as it was one of those rare sunny Saturday's, I would take Joyce and the two girls to Alki beach to go rollerblading. Alki is one of the few destination beaches on the Puget Sound. It has a two and a half mile long pedestrian walkway, and enjoys breathtaking views of Seattle, the Puget Sound, and the Olympic Mountains.

When we arrived, there must have been six games of beach volleyball being played. Kids were combing the beach for shells. The energy was contagious. We put on our skates and entered the pedestrian walkway. I was holding the hand of my eight-year old daughter, a pretty good skater, cruising down the sidewalk, when Emma hit a rock, immediately sending her into a freefall. I raised my hand to lift her in the air so she could regain her footing, but she was unsuccessful.

I then made the conscious decision to lift her one last time, as long as possible, to cushion her fall. I was successful. But instead of Emma alone hitting the pavement, we were both going down. She fell with barely a scratch. I was not so fortunate. I sprained my left wrist, bruised both my left elbow and my left butt cheek, and had to dig asphalt out of my right hand. It could have been worse, but I was still feeling the pain.

When I got home, I popped two Advil and made the decision not to take advantage of the Halloween night life and potential Halloween surge fares offered by Uber. At 7 pm, I got into bed and attempted to relax to no avail. It would be better to drive with some pain, rather than sit in bed and be constantly aware that my body was not healing at the rate of my former 40-year old, 30-year old, or 20-year old self.

By 7:30 pm, I was in my car, ready to greet Halloween revelers. By the time I hit the first light, I was tagged by a passenger. I picked up a young man and dropped him off at the Hyatt in downtown, less than a half a mile drive. I believe he was a little shocked by the short distance (about two blocks) as he did not want to get out of the car. I assured him we were at his destination, when one of the Hyatt Valet's came, and opened the car door for him. He reluctantly departed. I earned two dollars and sixty-two cents for 3 minutes and 20 seconds of work. My greedy friend Uber helped himself to three dollars and eighteen cents.

Scott and his Four-Year Old Daughter

I was immediately tagged by another passenger at the Cheesecake Factory, just down the street. I picked up Scott and his four-year old daughter. I offered Scott the use of the car seat I kept in the trunk. Scott declined.

Scott and his daughter were just coming out from dinner at the Cheesecake Factory. As they entered the car, I could see Scott was completely absorbed by his daughter, almost as if he had not seen her for a long time. The daughter, on the other hand, was totally absorbed with a Disney Halloween cartoon on her IPad. It felt like I could have jumped out of the car and they wouldn't have noticed. When Scott started to sing along with one of the songs playing on the iPad, his daughter told him, "Stop!" which he obediently did.

I started to think Scott's night out with his daughter was part of a parenting plan visit. I thought: Thursday and Friday nights are the usual nights when the non-custodial parent would get their one night to spend with their child, but maybe this family had the father take the daughter on a Saturday night.

As it was the dad and daughter's time, I stuck to driving. The father, worn down in his attempts to interact with his daughter, asked me, "How long will it take to reach the house?"

I looked at my app and said, "Another five minutes. By the way, from your accent, I am thinking you are from New York."

He laughed and said, "Yes, I grew up in New York, but have been living here for a while. The accent never leaves."

Scott's daughter set her iPad down, noticing her father was no longer paying attention to her. She looked at her father and said in a loud voice, "Are we doing anything next week?"

Scott said, "Of course," and asked why.

She responded, "No reason, I was just wondering."

Scott did not realize that his daughter still wanted his attention, even if it was "negative attention". The daughter interjected herself into our conversation because Scott's focus shifted from her to me. It seemed like a passive-aggressive approach by the daughter, something I seldom saw at so early an age. But at least for me, the daughter's need for her father's attention, positive or negative, was obvious. Whatever the cost, she wanted his full, undivided attention.

Just as I was pondering my amateur psychological analysis, we arrived at their residence. The house was about 1000 feet high on Cougar Mountain with breathtaking views of Seattle and the Olympics. Later, I went online and saw that the homes ranged from 1.5 million dollars to 4 million dollars. I pulled in front of a palatial house, got out of the car, and opened their door.

The two got out of the car, thanked me and walked to the garage. Scott attempted a key code which did not work. Finally, he went up to the front door and knocked. Not wanting to leave a dad and daughter stranded, I waited. But the father turned around and gave me an uncomfortable look. If I was right, he was dropping his daughter off at the mother's house. The door finally opened and the pair slipped into the house.

Darn, I was doing it again, waiting for someone to go inside. But I so wanted to yell to Scott, "Your daughter loves you! Everything is going to be all right." But I was an Uber driver. What did I know? I made maybe fifteen dollars per hour. I needed to move to the next passenger.

I did not have to wait long. There might not be a surge in pricing as promised, but at least there was no waiting as the calls were coming in, one after the other. Unfortunately, I was on my way to pick up my next passenger when the fare was cancelled. Uber compensated me three dollars and seventy-five cents.

Alyssa, the Alpha Female

My next passengers were three young girls headed to Seattle for a late-night dinner. Alyssa, the alpha female, shepherded her spirited friends into the car. As soon as the girls were seated, multiple fragrances immediately engulfed me.

The evening was not turning out as I hoped. It looked like I would not meet Halloween-clad passengers, and I would be regulated to strictly driving instead of the incredible conversations I had previously. But then again, I was here to drive, not engage.

The girls spent the entire ride going over love affairs, fights they had with each other and the difficulties of being single, oblivious to the fact that I was in the car. On the other hand, I was completely entertained by the sophomoric banter. I felt like a front seat voyeur, entertained by the back and forth banter.

The girls were beautiful and educated with a whole world of opportunity open to them. They were truly living and enjoying the moment. I made a mental note to educate my girls about appreciating what they have and a second mental note to educate my girts about being more discreet in front of strangers. I dropped off the young ladies in what looked to be promising nightlife at Pioneer Square. To my delight, the girls, on stepping out of the car, acknowledged my existence and thanked me for the ride, which I enjoyed more than a tip.

The Paramount

Feeling some pain due to my earlier fall, I was going to go back home when another passenger popped up. All right, I thought, I am in downtown Seattle, so one more attempt at some Halloween revelry. I picked up an attractive young couple on what looked like a date. They were dressed to the nines for some event, but were not talking to each other.

Their destination was the Paramount, a performing arts venue, just a mile away. The car was filled with an awkward silence. I could not help myself and asked if they were going to a play. The woman said they were going to see an off-Broadway production of Aladdin. As we were stuck in traffic, I turned around, made eye contact with both and said, "Wow, I cannot imagine a more enchanted evening." They both smiled and started talking about the play with each other. I felt like I was playing Cupid on Halloween.

After dropping the couple off, I sat quietly in my car and reflected on my evening. I did not have a lot of conversations and I did not get to see the highly anticipated costume-draped Halloween revelers, but sometimes, listening can be just as rewarding. I made three dollars and Uber made four dollars on my last ride. I made a total of forty-four dollars and sixty cents for less than two hours of work and one hundred and seventy-one dollars and twenty cents for the week (total of 6 hours, 19 minutes). If I took out fifty cents per mile, I was once again left asking, how in the world would drivers eke out a living.

That evening, Joyce presented me with a spreadsheet to track my Uber earnings. Joyce included some of the variables I created. For example, I decided to charge a flat rate of fifty cents per mile. The charge included gas, depreciation of the car, maintenance of the car, carwashes, and insurance. I used fifty cents from my experience with my past jobs. When I drove my personal vehicle for the college, I was reimbursed anywhere between forty-two cents a mile to fifty-eight cents a mile, so I believed I should at least be in the ballpark.

From this point on, I would be able to track the hours I worked, the costs I incurred, and my hourly rate of pay. Doing the math in my head, I wasn't optimistic. But with spreadsheet in hand, we would see. I would begin charting my earnings this Monday.

CHAPTER FOUR

DOES IT PAY?

How Can You Mend a Broken Heart?
October 30, 2017, Monday

Trips	Time on Road	Miles	Uber Earnings	Vehicle Cost	Real Earnings	Hourly Wage
6	2 hr 45 min	49	$57.31	-$24.50	$32.81	$11.93

Spreadsheet in hand, okay, on laptop, I was excited to start my day, and get my first look at my real earnings. By the time I finished driving, I would have all the information I needed to enter the numbers required to get at my hourly wage. I would know how many miles I drove by manually recording my starting and ending odometer readings. The Uber app would provide me with my total earnings for the day. And using my fifty cents a mile for wear and tear on the vehicle, the spreadsheet could then subtract my vehicle cost from my Uber earnings to show my real earnings, and than divide my real earnings by the number of minutes I worked to get my hourly wage. Thank you Excel and more specifically Joyce, for making these calculations automatic.

I was now ready to track my earnings. I turned on the app, wrote down the time, and entered the odometer reading of my car. It was a little difficult, as I juggled making my entries and driving at the same time, but my digital recorder would be arriving soon.

Joan

I picked up my first passenger, Joan, a woman in her late 50's or early 60's, at her apartment in front of Bellevue Square Park. Her destination was a radiology lab and I could tell she was not an employee. Joan was not wearing a uniform and appeared apprehensive.

I assumed Joan was going for tests, so I attempted to make light conversation. I said, "I pick up my two younger daughters from the bus stop at the park, so I walk past your building every afternoon. It is a new building, isn't it? I believe it came up at the same time they expanded the park across the street."

Joan seemed eager to engage me in conversation. She said, "Yes, we moved into the apartment a year and a half ago when the apartment building first opened. The construction going on at the park was horrible at the time, but now that the new, expanded park has opened, we really love it here."

While we were talking about the neighborhood, Joan suggested an alternative route through Bellevue's worse traffic. Any advice she offered, I followed. I thought what she needed at the moment was a sense of control. I thanked her for her navigational insights which made her smile. It caused enough of a distraction that by the time we arrived at the lab, she appeared more at ease.

I realized at that moment what a shallow human being I had become. Sometimes, I get too focused, and that morning, I became so preoccupied with my spreadsheet that I almost forgot my first mission, to take care of the passenger. I watched Joan get out of the car and walk into the building. I had half a mind to wait for her and drive her back home. But again, that would probably be creepy.

As I drove away, feeling somewhat blue, and maybe out of some sort of penance, I embarked on a record-breaking six trips. Unfortunately, I could not retain all of the stories. But the last two trips, which I did manage to write up, like the first trip, reminded me again and again that I was here to perform a service, as both trips were filled with sadness and quite possibly, broken hearts.

James

I found myself once again in Seattle, picking up a young couple, forlornly standing on 4th street, suitcases in hand. I got out of the car and quickly placed their bags in the trunk. When I returned to my seat, I was surprised to find James in the front seat and Marie in the back seat. They were not talking.

James was obviously frustrated. Regardless of the directions coming out of my speakerphone, James told me exactly where to go and when to go. I listened obediently, hoping my silence would provoke some conversation between the couple. With the exception of James giving me directions, utter silence. The tension in the car was wearing on me. I thought, well, maybe they are just work professionals sharing an Uber?

As the uncomfortable silence continued, I found myself speeding toward their location. Seattle's downtown area has numerous stoplights and when you catch one green light, you usually can catch a string of green lights which probably accounted for my error in judgment. I rushed through an intersection and ran a red light.

James was in the middle of giving me directions and immediately called out my indiscretion. "Hey, you just ran a red light."

I thought about being funny and saying, "The light was actually a burnt orange." But no, it was definitely red.

So, I deflected, "Fortunately, I have never received a traffic ticket."

James said, "That is good to know." He then went back to giving me directions.

Surprisingly, the next day, I believe James was responsible for my second ever Uber compliment. Passengers can provide both star ratings and give compliments to drivers. The compliment read, "All Star Driver". Maybe James thought of me more as an Indy race car driver? Regardless of the praise, it was the wrong thing to do, and I took a mental note in the hopes I would not repeat the transgression.

When I dropped the couple off at the front door of their apartment building on Seattle's north side, I unloaded their suitcases, got back into my car and made a U-turn. I glanced over at the couple who were standing, staring at each other in grim silence, not having moved from their bags. I opened my window and asked if they were okay. The woman looked relieved and replied with a smile, "We're fine." The social worker in me wanted to encourage them to break out of their shells and embrace each other. But, again… Uber driver.

Regine, Broken Heart

Before I could reach the intersection, I was called by my final fare of the day, a sad young woman who was trailing behind another woman. Regine appeared to be on the outs with her lover. I watched as Regine's girlfriend carried her suitcase and garment bag to the car which I then placed in the trunk. The girls gave each other a quick kiss goodbye. Regine, tears in her eyes, watched her girlfriend slowly walk away, maybe waiting for her to turn around and wave good-bye. Her girlfriend did not turn around.

The trip to Regine's place by Safeco Field felt pretty much like a funeral march. I asked if there was anything I could do and received a muffled, "No!"

When we arrived at her apartment, Regine stood silently at the back of my car, helpless as I pulled her bags out. She remained motionless, silently staring into the traffic. I asked her if she was going to be alright and she responded in the greatest of pain, "I'll be okay."

I wanted to give her a hug, but again… Uber driver. I waited five minutes, I know, creepy, until she finally picked up her bags and walked toward her apartment building. The world can be an awfully sad place. I wished I could have done more.

Regine would be my last drive for the day. I pulled over on the road, wrote down both my ending time and my odometer reading. I completed six trips and had some excellent data to plug into my spreadsheet.

When I got home, I saw that I made fifty-seven dollars and forty-one cents for just under three hours of work. Unfortunately, my costs were twenty-four dollars and fifty cents for net earnings of thirty-two dollars and eighty-one cents. My suspicions were correct. I earned eleven dollars and ninety-three cents an hour for my record-setting six trips. Regardless of my earnings, I felt immensely pleased with myself. What a wonderful, yet incredibly sad three hours.[7]

HALLOWEEN DAY
October 31, 2017, Tuesday

Trips	Time on Road	Miles	Uber Earnings	Vehicle Cost	Real Earnings	Hourly Wage
3	1 hr 41 min	46	$46.95	-$23.00	$23.95	$13.56

It might have been Halloween, but I had quite the international experience. Each of my three rides contained a passenger from a different continent.

Europe, Beautiful Nadia
I drove to the Bellevue Hyatt and a valet immediately approached my car. I've started to notice that the valets often mistake me for a

---

[7] Follow up Note: I finally took the time to see whether I could pick up passengers from SeaTac. I tried to text Uber and find out, but no response. I looked for an Uber driver help line, but could not find one. After a little more searching, I found the answer to my SeaTac question: "To meet environmental goals, the Port of Seattle will only allow Uber vehicles with a blended MPG rating of 45 or higher to pick up passengers at Sea-Tac." My car does not qualify so the answer to my question was a resounding no. I could drive passengers to SeaTac, but I couldn't bring passengers back from SeaTac. Unfortunately, when I picked up a passenger in Bellevue and brought them to the airport, I would be making a roundtrip drive for a one-way fare. We'd have to see what that meant financially the next time someone wanted a ride out to SeaTac. On a positive note, I finally found the Uber phone number in the app. I called to find out if I could block airport rides to SeaTac. I waited seven minutes, and when I finally got a human being on the line, English was not their first language. I struggled through the call and learned nothing new in regard to how to block SeaTac as a destination. My experience at the Hub, little to no training for passengers, and my call to the Uber help line, it was the first time I felt that maybe Uber was not my friend after all.

customer. I told the valet I was waiting to pick up Nadia, when out walked a beautiful, Eastern European woman. It was Nadia. I could tell the valet was impressed as he quickly moved past me and ran over to get the door for her. Nadia appeared incredibly anxious and completely ignored him.

Nadia told me she was going to Microsoft, so I started driving in the direction of Microsoft, only to find out the destination she entered was the Microsoft Campus. I had never seen this before and was immediately confused. I asked her, "Where are you heading to on the Microsoft campus?"

"Microsoft," she replied tersely. Nadia used Uber two years ago, the last time she was in the United States, and did not remember that she had to enter an address, which she did not have on her.

I let Nadia know that the Microsoft Campus was a lot like a small city. Nadia continued to feed me information in bits and pieces. "It's at the Microsoft Learning Center," she finally informed me.

I thanked her for the information. "Let me pull over in this mini-mall and I will check Google maps."

Nadia's anxiety seemed to grow as she responded, "Let's go back to the hotel as all the employees know where it is."

I ignored the obvious slight and found the location on Google maps. I enjoyed the irony that I had to use Google to get to Microsoft. I enjoyed further that Google ultimately took me to the wrong destination.

"I found the location," I announced. "Would you like me to turn around and go to the hotel to find directions from one of the employees?"

"No, let's go," she said abruptly. I took off to Microsoft, but ended up at the wrong end of the Microsoft Campus. I was picking up on a pattern. Every time I used Google to get to Microsoft, the directions were not always accurate.

I needed to get some directions and there were a couple of Microsoft employees, dressed in Halloween costumes, advertising a fundraising drive as employees drove onto campus. I told her I would ask them for directions to which she promptly replied, "They will not know."

This time, I quietly ignored her. I asked the man dressed as a big bunny for help. He gave me specific directions to the Microsoft Learning Center.

I do not like to see people agitated and I felt bad for Nadia. I assumed she travelled from eastern Europe and came to the Microsoft Campus for a workshop. Maybe Nadia did not realize how easy it would be for her to come into any room and immediately make everyone feel better by her mere presence. Instead, she projected a contagious anxiety.

When I finally got her to her destination with time to spare, I could tell she was still flustered. I wanted to say, "Hey, you have incredible presence. You will knock everyone off their feet lucky enough to meet you." But as an Uber driver, no matter how sincere the thought might be, it would be entirely inappropriate.

India, Halloween Party

I was feeling a little anxious from my trip with Nadia. Fortunately, my next call went much smoother as I picked up a mom and dad and their daughter. The daughter was dressed as a Ladybug, as the family was headed to a Montessori school for a Halloween program. The family was taking pictures of the festive bug as I drove up.

When the family situated themselves into the car, I complimented the girl on her costume and everyone beamed. The family proceeded to speak an Indian dialect over the short duration of the drive. I loved listening to them as celebrations have a way of drawing out the best in people, and whatever dialect from India they were speaking, it was beautiful. When I arrived at the Montessori school, I opened the car door for them and said goodbye.

The little girl hesitated at getting out of the car. When she finally got out, she said goodbye to me at least three times. My heart melted as the mother took her hand, presented me with the sweetest smile, and started to walk away with the little girl's eyes still following me. I love Halloween. For one day each year, people turn into anyone their heart desires. Regardless of where one comes from, it is as if we all become one family.

South America, Javier

I was running low on gas when I got tapped by Javier, my final passenger of the day. I picked Javier up at his Bellevue residence, and saw that he was going to SeaTac. On this occasion, given I had less than a quarter of a tank of gas, I knew I would be cutting it close.

As soon as Javier stepped into the car, he got on the phone and began a conversation that lasted the entire trip. The call was in Spanish, so I attempted to see how much Spanish I could recall. Given traffic, I abandoned my translation efforts and instead, sat back and enjoyed the sound of his laughter. It was a business call, but whoever was on the line, they said enough things to keep him properly amused.

At SeaTac, Javier stepped out of the car, still talking on his phone. I knew I had a long drive back in pretty heavy traffic, but Javier rubbed off on me. I was now in a good mood, delighted by both Javier's contagious laughter and the diverse group of passengers I had the privilege to enjoy.

Later, when I got home, I saw that I made a new high on the hourly wage front, thirteen dollars and fifty-six cents per hour. As I looked at the numbers, the SeaTac trip was a big factor in my earnings. I thought, maybe the round-trip expense for a one-way trip was worth it? I also saw two more compliments: "All Star Driver" and "Excellent Service". It is amazing how low wages look almost glowing when coupled with flattery.

Terrorism

November 1, 2017, Wednesday

A parent-teacher conference and two wellness checks for the girls meant no Uber today. Then, the news reports came in about the terrorist attack in New York. Sayfullo Saipov, the father of three, killed eight people and injured twelve more in New York City in the name of ISIS.

Sayfullo and I had two things in common: we were Uber drivers and we had a family. So as a fellow driver, I thought long and hard about how this 29-year old man with a family could commit such a heinous act.

A graduate of Tashkent Financial Institute, one of the largest universities in Uzbekistan, Sayfullo moved to the United States where he hoped to make his fortune. Sayfullo was reported to have driven over 1,400 trips for Uber over the past six months. That would mean Sayfullo worked backbreaking hours to support a wife and three children on thirty thousand dollars to forty thousand dollars per year (and that includes overtime) in one of the nation's most expensive cities.

I could not begin to imagine what it would be like for an educated, young immigrant to try to support a family in a high cost bedroom community outside of New York City on an Uber income. In my own situation, I had privilege and power on my side. I was not afraid of the police, and the few times I was pulled over by the police, I drove away with a warning. I had full confidence when I stepped out of a car, I was not going to be shot. If I was a person of color or a man with a large beard in Islamic dress, would I be so certain?

I was also pretty sure that being a poorly paid "taxi" driver in the United States was not one of Sayfullo's dreams when attending the university in Uzbekistan. My conclusion, at least at this point in my Uber experience, was that Sayfullo Saipov, driving for Uber, was not living the American dream.

No one doubted that Sayfullo needed to feel the full weight of the law. Sayfullo allowed himself to become radicalized, so he, and his family, were now going to pay for his actions. On the other hand, for the purposes of this narrative, Sayfullo's story was just another illustration that the pursuit of the American Dream needed a lot more than Uber.

HOLY SMOKE
November 2, 2017, Thursday

Trips	Time on Road	Miles	Uber Earnings	Vehicle Cost	Real Earnings	Hourly Wage
2	20 min	9	$8.40	-$4.50	$3.90	$11.70

Shawn

I picked up my first fare, Shawn, at the downtown Residence Inn. He entered the car, talking on his phone, and stayed on the phone the entire ride. What makes people discuss the most intimate details of their life in front of a stranger?

I turned off Sirius so Shawn could talk undisturbed without the static sound of music in the background. It was not a business meeting. Shawn was making a confession. All I could think was, way too much information. As my ears burned, I thought seriously about testing my car's Bing speakers.

Shawn was disclosing to his buddy what was taking place in his court-ordered marriage counseling. He was "voluntarily" participating in counseling for his daughter's sake. He didn't say anything negative about his wife, but he didn't say anything positive.

According to Shawn, his wife did most of the heavy emotional lifting in the relationship. I thought it was good that Shawn owned that until he told his friend: "But that is not me. And I have to be me."

Shawn felt the counseling was a win/win. If the family divorced, counseling would show that Shawn tried. The real intent? Counseling was Shawn's ticket to get his wife to come back even after his "transgressions". As to further transgressions, he wasn't going to change.

As he reflected on his situation, Shawn became slightly enraged, saying counseling was "just horse shit." But Shawn was an opportunist. If he could play his cards right, he could leave the right impression without having to actually do anything. I thought, what a bastard! I wouldn't be surprised if his wife had the @METOO hashtag.

I was used to driving people I came to respect. Given the terrorist attack committed by an Uber car driver yesterday and now this disclosure by a passenger, I was relieved when Shawn got out of the car. It was the first time I actually wanted to push someone out of the car.

Donald

Donald, my next passenger, would also be my last passenger of the day. Driving up the long street leading to a seedy apartment complex, I saw Donald standing just off the curb, smoking a cigarette. Maybe Donald was karma and I was being punished by my ugly thoughts about my last passenger.

Bummer, I thought. He's a smoker.

Donald was my first smoker. When Donald saw me, he threw his cigarette to the ground and got into the car. My senses were immediately assaulted by the smoldering chimney now sitting in my back seat. Some people smoke, but do a good job controlling the smell. Donald was not one of those people. I found myself, for the second time in a row, feeling assaulted by my passengers. The first assault came in the guise of manipulation, lies, and deception. The second assault came in the form of toxic chemicals.

The destination, what looked like an abandoned strip mall, was a little over a mile and took just only three minutes and fifty seconds. The smell was so bad, it felt more like thirty minutes. Donald did not say a word, but I could tell he was agitated. Donald fidgeted in the back seat the entire way.

As soon as Donald stepped out of the car, I breathed a sigh of relief. Unfortunately, the smell of smoke was still heavy in the car. I turned off my app and continued to drive with my windows opened in the hope of clearing the smell. Cigarette smoke seeped into everything. The smell was not about to leave my car. There was no way I was going to pick up passengers in a car that smelled like an ashtray. I called it a day.

I returned home, went online, and ordered 4 car deodorizers. The two dollars and ninety-two cents I earned from Donald's fare did not make up for the fourteen dollars and ninety-five cents it cost for the deodorizer four pack. I earned just over eight dollars for the entire day. Subtract the fourteen dollars and ninety-five cents for the deodorizers, I ended the day seven dollars out of pocket. That being said, the deodorizers were worth the investment. Donald would not be my last smoker.

SNOWFALL
November 3, 2017, Friday

Trips	Time on Road	Miles	Uber Earnings	Vehicle Cost	Real Earnings	Hourly Wage
3	1 hr 5 min	11	$17.86	-$5.50	$12.36	$11.41

My digital recorder arrived and I was psyched. I had not used a recorder since college and at that time, I was using microcassettes. It took about two minutes to get familiar with the new technology and I was ready. I thought it would have been handy to have had the digital recorder yesterday to record Shawn's conversation and then send it over to his wife. But that would not have happened anyway. I was not going to betray the confidence of my passenger. I already committed to not recording rides; just recording notes.

Today was an unusual day, as Seattle rarely averages 6 inches of snow for the entire year. Here we were in early November, and a light dusting of snow was on the ground. For my girls, it might as well have been Christmas. They excitedly pointed to snow on top of cars that were kept out overnight, not having the benefit of a garage or shelter.

As we waited for the bus, I turned on the Uber app and saw that surge pricing was in effect for Bellevue. I recently let Julia and Emma in on my Uber project, so I pointed to the red area on the app that highlighted Bellevue and said, "Look, surge pricing."

Squeezing into the front seat, they asked, "What does that mean?"

I explained to them, "Surge pricing means demand is greater. There are probably more people in need of rides than drivers, so drivers get more money. The red area means surge pricing is now in effect and drivers in the red area will benefit with higher rates."

"So, if you go now," Julia asked, "you will get more money?"

"Yes," I acknowledged.

Julia and Emma became excited and told me to go.

I pointed my finger back at the app and said, "Look, in the brief time it took me to explain surge pricing, the red color overlaying Bellevue has now turned orange. In a matter of moments, the surge pricing will be gone."

The girls could not conceal their disappointment, "Come on, Dad, there is still time. You can still go."

When some other parents showed up at the bus stop and the girls were no longer alone, they pleaded with me to go, as if hoping I would win some type of lottery. Finally, I gave in and went back to the car, only to see the surge pricing, as I predicted, vanished. I got back out of the car and returned to where the girls were waiting. I reported the news to my daughters' disappointment. But… Uber had now become a source of family fun.

Tomoko

My first passenger was Tomoko. I turned on the digital recorder, stated Tomoko's name aloud, and then spelled it. Good start.

Tomoko, probably in her late thirties, elegant and smartly dressed, was from Seoul. She just flew into Seattle, but was both kind and talkative. We were on our way to the Microsoft Campus when she caught sight of the light snowfall that dusted the ground. She rarely saw snow and even though there was little snow to be seen, was overcome with excitement. I heard a loud "Ahhhh! Snow," almost like an excited school girl.

Hearing someone get excited by winter's first snowfall was a heart-warming experience, and it came at the right time. The leaves already turned and would soon be completely gone from the trees. I was mourning the passing of my favorite season. Turning around and looking at Tomoko's astonished face at Seattle's first snowfall, I found myself now looking forward to winter.

I asked Tomoko, "How long are you staying in the area?"

She responded, "Ten days."

"There are a few places in the mountains close by where you can literally bathe in snow. If you like, I can write down some of the locations for you."

"I am working during the day, and as the sun is setting earlier and earlier, I will have to wait until my next visit to Seattle. Would you be able to drive me the next time I am out?"

I was caught off guard, but responded: "Sure."

What I was thinking was an entirely different matter. Can I drive someone outside of Uber? Is it professional? Why does this feel so uncomfortable? Or was she asking if she used Uber again, could she request me? Okay, stay professional.

When we arrived at Microsoft, I provided my name to Tomoko. Would I hear from her and what would I say if I was no longer driving? It didn't matter. As I drove back to Bellevue, I couldn't get the silly smile off my face.

Ludovick

Once I reached downtown Bellevue, I was tagged to pick up Ludovick. Ludovick was waiting outside with another man, two large suitcases in hand. I took their suitcases and placed them in the trunk of the car. I then opened the door for them. Ludovick was highly impressed. I probably had an extra bounce in my step due to my last passenger.

Both men, Microsoft employees, spoke English with heavy eastern European accents. With the exception of a couple of sentences in their native tongue, most probably Russian, they spoke in English. I enjoyed listening to them strategize about how to complete a project for their manager at Microsoft.

When I arrived at the Microsoft Campus, I took their suitcases out of the trunk and pulled up the retractable handles so they were ready when they got out of the car. With a big smile on his face, Ludovick said, "Thank you for being so professional." It is funny how a compliment can make one's day.

Shana

Feeling empowered by the compliment, I decided to do one more ride. It had to be a little after 10 am and the call came from one of the healthcare facilities at Overlake Hospital in Bellevue. I arrived at a radiology lab and picked up Shana.

Shana was standing curbside with a frown on her face. I jumped out of the car to get the door for Shana and the frown turned into a grin from ear to ear. There must have been something in the air. Where yesterday seemed like a disaster, today was more than making up for yesterday's experiences.

Shana was an employee at Expedia and I assumed she completed taking some tests. She sat quietly in the car. I did not want to disturb her and left her to her thoughts.

When I arrived at Expedia, a block from my home, I had to double park. Shana got out of the car, but did not fully shut the door. She turned to me with a panicked expression, realizing too late she did not fully shut the door. I gave her a thumbs-up, letting her know through an assortment of gestures that felt like a game of charades, that I knew the door was not shut and I would take care of it. I drove slowly for a block and a half until I made it to my parking garage, got out of the car, and made sure the back door was fully shut.

What a day! For an hour and five minutes, I witnessed a Korean woman's first glimpse of Seattle's early snowfall, I was the recipient of a man's recognition of my good manners, and, I had the opportunity to create a warmer environment for a woman that appeared stressed about medical tests or possibly her workplace. Sharing snowfall, putting away a suitcase, and opening a door were more than a service; they were acts of care. In such a short period of time, I realized that even strangers can touch each other's lives in small, meaningful ways. And… I now had a digital recorder to ensure I captured as many details as possible.

Replaced?

November 4, 2017, Saturday

I don't drive on Saturday, but I did happen to come across a piece of news that alarmed me. The first article was Stephen Hawking's prediction that robots are nearer than anyone thought in replacing humans at work.[8] So, it was not surprising when I followed up Hawking's prediction with an article on Uber's next generation of self-driving cars. Uber's self-driving cars could be on the road as early as the end of this year.[9]

Next generation? I didn't even know there was a first generation of self-driving cars. I did an internet search and found that Uber's first generation of self-driving cars were introduced in Pittsburgh over a year ago.[10]

Uber's cars may be self-driving, but two people still sit in the front of the car. The first Uber employee sits in the driver's seat and takes control if there is trouble with the self-driving feature. The second Uber employee sits in the passenger seat and monitors the performance of the vehicle.

One of Uber's hardware engineers said the company is close to having no vehicle operators. Wow! It really did look like my foray into Uber driving might end quicker than I thought. I must admit, I was a little hurt at the thought of being outsourced by a self-driving vehicle. I thought of myself as a value add to the Uber transportation service.

But with a little more reflection, I imagined I could be easily replaced. The next generation of Uber cars will most likely be equipped with Uber's equivalent of Amazon's Alexa or Apple's Siri. The passenger could step into the car, request to control the temperature, watch a movie or pick a selection of songs, or even request a conference call. At least for today, it felt like Stephen Hawking was a prophet.

---

[8] http://fortune.com/2017/11/03/stephen-hawking-danger-ai/

[9] http://www.foxnews.com/auto/2017/11/03/uber-prepares-next-generation-self-driving-cars.html

[10] https://www.npr.org/sections/alltechconsidered/2017/04/03/522099560/pittsburgh-offers-driving-lessons-for-ubers-autonomous-cars

There was one piece of good news, and it came in the introduction of a new service called Gobi.[11] When I am replaced by a robot, I could always become a babysitter. Gobi, which many call "Uber for Babysitters", provides on-demand sitters. Gobi hopes to fill the demand for families when mom or Dad are called away unexpectedly. Babysitters, like drivers for Uber, can be rated. I believe we have a long time before we see babysitting robots. But then again, I thought it would take much longer for the self-driving car.

---

[11] http://www.abc.net.au/news/2017-11-05/uber-for-babysitters-future-of-childcare-or-step-too-far/9063068

CHAPTER FIVE

HONEYMOON PERIOD

HOLY DAY
November 5, 2017, Sunday

Trips	Time on Road	Miles	Uber Earnings	Vehicle Cost	Real Earnings	Hourly Wage
3	1 hr 30 min	39	$43.95	-$19.50	$20.50	$13.67

I thought it might be interesting to see what type of business I would do on a Sunday afternoon. Okay, I saw surge pricing (weather-related), and decided to take advantage of the opportunity, but by the time I made it to the street, the surge pricing was gone, of course. It was also a day of unusual weather. For the second time this fall, Seattle was experiencing light snowfall.

A lot of people in the Seattle area are not used to driving in the snow. So, I was not surprised when my first fare was 17 miles away at the outskirts of Redmond. Was the seventeen-mile trek to pick up a passenger worth the fare? I decided I would find out.

Indira

I picked up Indira, who needed a ride that took only six minutes and twenty-three seconds to get her to her destination, the Redmond Public Library. Because the fare was seventeen miles away, I believed

Uber would reimburse me for the time it took me to reach Indira. Not the case.

I earned four dollars and forty-two cents for the ride. The cost to travel just to the pick-up point alone was eight dollars and fifty cents (fifty cents per mile). So, I lost four dollars and eight cents even before I began the seven plus minute trip to the library.

Okay, maybe I was being unfair. Maybe fifty cents per mile for gas, oil, maintenance and depreciation was too high. I needed to find a more objective standard. I went online to find out the mileage reimbursement rate for Washington State employees. The answer: fifty-three cents per mile, three point five cents per mile more than my documented reimbursement number. Okay, I was well in the ballpark with my reimbursement rate when I established fifty cents per mile. Unfortunately, given the high cost associated with driving, this meant drivers really needed to be careful about which fares they accepted. Driving seventeen miles in mostly city traffic to pick up a passenger was not a wise business choice.

The fare aside, Indira, my passenger, was delightful. When I got out and opened the door for her, she asked if it was okay for her to sit in the front seat. I said of course, closed the back door and opened the front door. She smiled and got in.

We started to talk about the book collection at the Redmond Library. Several books were on the floor of the front seat which she noticed. Indira picked up one of the books, "Books on Irish folktales? That's pretty interesting."

I told her, "I'm writing a book based on a collection of Irish folktales compiled by W.B. Yeats."

She was completely fascinated, which as an author, is like instant flattery. And, like myself, she loved libraries. When we arrived at the library, I did not want the conversation to end. It was not often, whether driving or even in my personal life, that I am paired with another person who shares a passion for libraries.

As Indira walked away, I thought, I wish the government reimbursed drivers to take people to the library at the public's cost. It is something I would volunteer to do.

Then the thought struck me: Didn't I just do just that?

In the end, I concluded that I made a five-dollar contribution to bring someone to the library. I could live with that. It felt good.

Sai

Sai, my final passenger, had a heavy accent and, interestingly enough, was a mirror of myself. Sai too had a daughter attending the University of Washington, and a son, a junior in high school, who was currently applying for colleges. His son received the remarkable ACT score of 35 – an IVY League score. Yet, his son was studying to retake the test in the hopes of getting a 36.

My stepdaughter, a senior in high school, received a 33 on the ACT. Although a competitive score, it would be a steeper hill for her to climb in her application process to elite schools. Joyce asked her to retake the test, but unlike Sai's son, she was comfortable with a 33.

Both children had their hearts set on tier one schools. Sai's son wanted to go to MIT while my daughter had her heart set on Stanford. While Sai's son was involved in extracurricular activities like karate and violin, my daughter was the president of various school organizations, and was selected to go to Florida to perform in the national honor band (flute). Both children would do well.

Sai was heading out to Houston and we were rerouted to I-5 rather than I-405, due to inclement weather. It was the first time the Uber app took me to SeaTac via Seattle and I could tell it was a first for Sai, as he looked a little nervous about the longer route. The nervousness did not last long. We had an extra twenty minutes to wax proudly about our two children.

I dropped off Sai and we wished each other well. The ride had the perk of a little bonding time between two proud parents and I earned forty dollars. The ride back, however, was terrible. On a rainy day, driving back in heavy traffic from SeaTac without a passenger, I found my enthusiasm slowly slip away as I waited in gridlock.

I did pick up one fare on my way back home. The ride was a quick five-minute trip from a hotel in Renton to a restaurant. The battery on my cell phone was at eight percent as the charger on the iPhone dock stopped working. I would have to end the day after only three trips, or risk having my phone dying en route.

It did make me aware how reliant I became on my GPS. I couldn't recall the last time I used a printed map. Could I even read and interpret a map today?

A problem for another day. Sunday had some enjoyable rides, but I only earned a little over thirteen dollars per hour. If it were not for the long ride to the airport, the daily rate could easily have been closer to ten dollars per hour. But, overall, the day was good. I made a small amount of money, I bonded with another parent, and I performed a public service.

I had now completed almost a full month of Uber driving. The experience was more than I could have hoped for. Maybe I was getting better at listening, but passengers continued to weave and reveal interesting stories, if not experiences. Every day, I found myself eager to start driving.

Wages were certainly an issue. There was little research on what drivers actually earn. After one month, I concluded that Uber was an "okay" part-time wage. I have heard drivers making claims of making twenty-five dollars to thirty-five dollars per hour. Given my spreadsheet, it does not appear possible. Unfortunately, most drivers, and I am making a big assumption, look at the total earnings and do not take out their costs when talking about how much they really make. So, there was a social element that definitely needed to be addressed for people trying to eke out a full time, livable wage. My limited experience told me so far, driving was not a livable wage.

And still, I had to admit, I was addicted. In the precarious world of autonomous vehicles, I became in love with the ride share experience. I awaited eagerly to hear the story of my next passenger. I looked forward to having the opportunity to provide even the tiniest service in the hopes of lightening my passengers' load. Passengers might bury themselves in their cell phone, return trips from the airport were often solitary and long, but there was always the occasional view of Mount Rainer and the glorious landscape of the Pacific Northwest. I was officially on my Uber honeymoon.

LANGUAGE BARRIER
November 6, 2017, Monday

Trips	Time on Road	Miles	Uber Earnings	Vehicle Cost	Real Earnings	Hourly Wage
1	48 min	11	$17.17	-$5.50	$11.67	$14.59

Shanti and Her Granddaughter

Monday started with another challenge associated with working with a faceless boss. I arrived at a downtown apartment in Bellevue and opened the door for Shanti and her beautiful granddaughter. The destination was the granddaughter's school, the Eton Academy in Bellevue. Shanti spoke very little English, but no matter, I had the destination on the app and would get them there in short order. It appeared simple and a great start to what was a great previous week.

As I drove, Shanti and her daughter conversed in Hindi. About a minute from the destination, Shanti asked me, again in broken English, "Please wait 10 minutes at the school, I will need a ride back to the apartment."

Her granddaughter began to repeat what her grandmother said in English in case I did not understand. I turned around, smiled, and said to the two of them, "I understand."

What I did not understand was how Uber would compensate me, or if they would even compensate me for waiting. The faceless boss was hard to reach in emergencies, much less trying to get in touch with someone to find the path out of my current predicament. As I wanted to be of service to Shanti, I would just leave the clock running on the app and take her back to the apartment. Would Uber charge for my waiting and the return trip? I had no idea.

Shanti returned about five minutes later. Her first question to me when she got into the car was whether I spoke Hindi. I said, "I wish" with a smile. I might not make any money off this fare, but once again, I had the opportunity to both learn more about the workings of Uber and enjoy this grandmother/granddaughter relationship at the same time.

I dropped Shanti off, ended the ride and saw that I made seventeen dollars and seventeen cents for the ride. With vehicle costs, that worked out to almost fifteen dollars per hour, making it my best hourly wage to date. Thank you, Shanti! What was happening to me? I was getting excited because I almost made fifteen dollars per hour. Fifteen dollars an hour is the minimum wage in Seattle. It must be love.

Uber to the Rescue: Human Trafficking

I cut my day short to attend a previously scheduled doctor's appointment. Waiting in the doctor's office, I read how an Uber driver from Philadelphia saved a woman from human trafficking.[12] Wow, an Uber superhero, and so, the honeymoon continued.

According to the article, a woman was forced into sex with as many as thirty men a day. The girl's handlers called for an Uber and set the woman's destination to her hotel. When the Uber arrived, they made sure the young lady got into the car. As the driver pulled away, the woman began to break down, telling the driver she wanted to go to the police. The driver immediately flagged down a Pennsylvania state trooper who later credited the Uber driver with saving the girl's life. The handlers were arrested, and bail was posted at fifty thousand dollars and one million dollars respectively.

Driving itself involved risk. The Uber driver did not have to step into what became a potentially a dangerous situation. Yet, he called the police, and placed himself between the woman and her handlers. I realized I had been taking my work too lightly. Even without stepping into the middle of a dangerous situation, there were risks I was not considering each day I stepped into the car.

Taxi drivers, according to the US Occupational Safety and Health Administration, are 20 more times more likely to be murdered on the job than other workers.[13] And although there have been few reports of

---

[12] http://www.phillymag.com/news/2017/11/06/uber-driver-human-trafficking-victim/

[13] https://www.wired.com/2016/03/uber-lyft-can-much-keep-drivers-safe/

drivers being attacked by their passengers, incidents like a Taco Bell Executive beating his driver, a complete stranger riddling an Uber driver's car with bullets, and a Miami doctor that attempted to kick his driver before trashing his car still occured.[14]

I have now come across a number of stories where the driver played the hero and the victim. But for the most part, I read stories where drivers, trying to make a living or supplement a living, acted in a way that demonstrated the best in all of us. Although I needed to pay more attention to the risks of driving, I found myself, outside of the low hourly wage, taking great pride in this profession.

---

[14] https://www.wired.com/2016/03/uber-lyft-can-much-keep-drivers-safe/

CHAPTER SIX

DOUBTS

THEFT
November 7, 2017, Tuesday

Trips	Time on Road	Miles	Uber Earnings	Vehicle Cost	Real Earnings	Hourly Wage
3	1 hr 50 min	46	$34.81	-$23.00	$11.81	$6.44

Roberto

I picked up Roberto at the Residence Inn in Bellevue. Early 30's, impeccably dressed, I had a hard time identifying his dialect as Roberto previously lived in Italy, London, and Australia. In the United States, Roberto lived in New York, with his current home in Los Angeles. Roberto loved Los Angeles.

Roberto's first question out of the gate was, "What do you have on your agenda for the day?"

That was a first as passengers rarely asked me about my day out of the gate. I told him, "Today is filled with my girls' activities. After school, I will take them to piano lessons, then gymnastics."

A true renaissance man, Roberto started asking me about my Uber experience. He said, "I would have loved to have driven for Uber while in college. Uber is a win-win both for the passenger trying to get a decent transportation fare and the driver who can earn a decent wage."

"For myself," I said, "Uber provides a couple of extra dollars and some time outside of the house. But for the most part, it is not the win-win one might think, especially if someone is trying to make a living out of driving. I've started to use a spreadsheet to track my earnings to get a better picture."

"So, what is the hourly rate?"

"I make between ten dollars and fifteen dollars per hour, which is not a sustainable wage for the area. If you are doing this part-time and need money to help with a car payment, it certainly helps. But as a full-time profession, you would have to work long hours and then, most probably, you would only just get by."

Roberto was surprised. I would have loved to have heard his thoughts later that day when I discovered I made only six dollars and sixty-four cents an hour. I asked Roberto, "Did you hear about the Uber driver that was robbed?"

"No," he responded, looking interested.

"Well," I continued. "A teenage girl, just as the driver was pulling up to her destination, looked directly into his surveillance cam, reached her hand into his tip jar, and stole all his tip money."

"No," Roberto gasped.

"I know," I said. "I didn't even realize you could place a tip jar in the car. But given the low wages, and if this is the sole income this guy has to support a family, how does he not? It's bad enough the wages are low and then, adding insult to injury, someone comes along and steals from the poor guy. It reminds me of someone that lands an extra punch on someone already falling to the ground."

Roberto wholeheartedly agreed. Roberto was good. He had an easy-going manner that made one feel comfortable in opening up. Roberto then asked, "So, why are you really driving?"

Although I never disclosed why I was driving to any of my passengers, I decided to open up to Roberto, "I am writing a book about my experiences driving. I'm calling it *Diary of an Uber Driver*. But I have to tell you, I really love driving. I meet interesting people like yourself every day. While the pay is minimal, the stories are extraordinary."

Roberto, a big smile on his face, said in what sounded like a sincere voice, "I can't wait to read it."

I still think Roberto was being polite. I smiled, not at the compliment, but at Roberto. This young man had obviously come far in life and was going to go a lot farther. He was the first passenger that stepped into my car, more interested in my story than his own. He was an excellent listener and had strong empathy.

I would have loved to have heard more about his own story, but we reached the AT&T campus. Before stepping out of the car, Roberto asked, "Please tell me your full name so that when your book comes out, I do not miss it."

"Absolutely," I said. "Raymond Nadolny. And Roberto, the pleasure was mine. I will most likely change the names in the book, but I will certainly include a story about this ride. Thank you." Before I could even start recording my notes, I was on my way back to the Residence Inn to pick up another passenger.

Nandini

Nandini, my next fare, seemed to be in a hurry. Like Roberto, Nandini was another consultant headed to T-Mobile. As soon as she entered the car, she opened her computer and got to work.

On the way to the T-Mobile campus (a trip I now made three times), I made a wrong turn and apologized. She smiled and said, "I get so frustrated when the computer tells me which lane to go into. Then I become confused and miss the turn." She then turned to her phone where she remained for the rest of the ride.

I was surprised. Not only did Nandini recognize my frustration, but she took the time to step away from her work, empathize with my mistake, even though it extended her trip by a couple of minutes. I never knew what to expect on these trips. Maybe that was why I got up every morning, looking forward to the next adventure.

Jon

My next fare came up as soon as I dropped Nandini off. Jon, who lived in Bellevue, was on his way to SeaTac to catch a flight to LA. I told him, "Earlier today, I had a passenger who lives in LA, and was doing consulting work in Bellevue. Wow, does he love LA."

Jon laughed. Jon lived in Chicago in the Byrn Mawr area, a beautiful lakefront area on Chicago's north side, and was familiar with extreme weather. He pointed to all the colors on the trees and said, "I'm highly doubtful Los Angeles has all of these beautiful colors." After a little more conversation on the pros and cons of the Seattle area, we both came to the conclusion that Los Angles had the advantage when it came to weather.

The trip was largely uneventful until we arrived at SeaTac. Jon was on his phone making arrangements to be picked up at the airport in Los Angeles. I was deciding whether to end my day. And then, out of nowhere, it happened.

If you live in the Seattle area, you know how rare it is to see Mount Rainer, our local celebrity volcano, usually hidden by the clouds. When we drove up to the airport on this cloudy Tuesday, to my surprise, there stood Mount Rainer in all its brilliance. I literally shouted, "Look, you can see Mount Rainer."

There was a pause. Then I heard, in a loud voice: "Oh my God, Mount Rainer."

I said to Jon, "When you are in Los Angeles, and if you start thinking about moving there, remember that picture." Wow, two adult men completely undone by such majesty. A truly Seattle experience… Every time Mount Rainer graces us with her presence, the experience is always awesomely stunning.

I was feeling pretty good about the three drives, that is, until I got home. Because of the distance I travelled and the two relatively short trips, I ended with my lowest hourly rate to date: six dollars and forty-four cents per hour, lower than minimum wage. The tip jar was starting to look good.

Later that night, I took my ten-year old daughter, Julia, to gymnastics. When I dropped Julia off, I took the opportunity to fill the car up with gas. When I finished, the final bill was just under fifty dollars. I was again reminded about the cost of driving. I returned to watch my daughter's practice, but the costs weighed heavily on my mind. Was the honeymoon period ending?

Maybe, I thought, Lyft, Uber's competitor, pays more. I had been hearing a lot of positive things about Lyft. If I became a Lyft driver, I could compare Uber to Lyft. I went online, searched for Lyft, and found Lyft was running a promotion where after the first 200 drives, the driver would receive five hundred dollars. Nice! I doubted I would ever reach 200 drives but it certainly provided incentive to do more drives.

It took about thirty minutes to complete most of the application process. All I needed to do was schedule a Lyft car inspection. The five-hundred dollar incentive offered by Lyft was certainly a step in the right direction.

TICKED OFF
November 8, 2017, Wednesday

Trips	Time on Road	Miles	Uber Earnings	Vehicle Cost	Real Earnings	Hourly Wage
3	1 hr 29 min	29	$29.96	-$14.81	$15.46	$10.42

Janet

Coffee in hand, I picked up my first fare, Janet, a sales person from Cleveland. As she stepped into the car, the first words poured unfiltered out of her mouth, "I hate my hotel. The customer service is terrible. The girl doesn't know what she is doing. I ordered a car thirty minutes ago and it never came. Now I am going to be late."

Janet was definitely on a tear. I smiled at her and said, "Sit back and do not worry. I will get you to the Meydenbauer Center (Bellevue's convention center) lickety-split."

Janet was not impressed by my optimism. Instead, her laundry list of complaints continued. She said, "I am not going to pay that hotel. That girl at the front desk was so rude. If they think that I am going to pay for that room, they are wrong. And… my presentation materials for my show never arrived. How can I present my product without any giveaways?"

I said in a positive voice, "You will take care of the hotel situation when you get back. And your product is probably so exceptional that you don't need giveaways." She laughed. I could tell she was beginning to thaw out, maybe even relax a little.

"You know what is going to happen?" she asked rhetorically, "We are going to drink all night with clients, get drunk and start again tomorrow."

"That sounds fun," I said.

"Not really. I really need a break. I have not taken a day off in three months. And I am not sure my boss is going to understand that I am at this show with no materials." Janet paused. "You know what?"

"What?"

"I am going to take Friday off."

"That is perfect," I said. "Friday is Veteran's Day so it is typically a slow business day." I pulled up to the front door of the Meydenbauer Center. The ride took six minutes and forty-two seconds, but in that short period of time, Janet seemed to be able to breathe again.

She opened the door to get out, paused, turned to me and said, "You know, I expected to be picked up in a GMC and was delighted when I saw you drive up in a Chrysler 300. Thank you so much for the ride."

"You're welcome," I said with a big smile on my face. "And given the start of your day, things will only get better. You will do great!" Janet hesitated, as if she wanted to say something more, and then quickly turned and walked away.

I almost yelled, "Go kick some ass today, Janet!" But I was an Uber driver, soon to be a Lyft driver, and that would be kind of creepy.

Uktash and Ben

Another fare popped up immediately. I picked up Uktash in downtown Bellevue and once again was on my way to the Microsoft Campus. There was a language barrier so we exchanged only a few informal greetings. It was somewhat of a relief as I was still attempting to absorb the impact of my drive with Janet.

I took one last passenger, Ben, a young man travelling from downtown Bellevue to Seattle. Once again, Ben had his head buried in his cell phone, so I was left alone with my thoughts. After I dropped Ben off in Pioneer Square, I waited five minutes. With no other calls, I returned home. There was a lot to reflect upon.

Driving really had become addictive? Why? I had theory.

My experience was that at least one passenger out of three would be incredibly interesting or entertaining. Driving became sort of like the lottery, where I kept buying a ticket and eventually I won something, however small. The excitement did not come from the money, but from just winning. Winning here was all about establishing a relationship, no matter how short the length of time I spent with the passenger. And that one passenger out of three always taught me something or made me reflect about my life or life in general.

This morning was a good example. I encountered a generational difference with Ben, and a language barrier with Uktash, so the connections with these passengers were limited. But once again, based on my one of out of three passenger experiences, I had a meaningful and what felt like a significant experience with Janet. Janet, for six minutes and forty-two seconds, went from anger to relief. She was provocative, engaging and ultimately human. By listening, I provided her with someone to confess to, someone to pour out her anger. I became an outlet with a safe venue for Janet to unload and then adjust her attitude in a positive way. The ride with Janet might have been an emotional roller coaster, but in a short period of time, we bonded.

THE NEW RECRUIT
November 9, 2017, Thursday

Trips	Time on Road	Miles	Uber Earnings	Vehicle Cost	Real Earnings	Hourly Wage
4	1 hr 19 min	20	$34.83	-$10.00	$24.83	$18.86

In Pittsburgh, Uber operates self-driving cars. And as of yesterday, Google launched its first autonomous shuttle in Las Vegas.[15] The autonomous shuttle's maiden voyage was followed immediately by a fender bender with a delivery truck. Score one for the human driver! Unfortunately, not. When the police officer arrived, the ticket did not go to the autonomous vehicle, but to the driver in the delivery truck. The day of the autonomous vehicle was looking like it was just around the corner.

That got me to thinking about how many people could lose their jobs when the autonomous cars eventually take over. There were 239,000 taxi cab drivers in the United States. Uber and Lyft had nearly overtaken that number with a combined 260,000 drivers. In New York City, there were more Uber drivers (14,088) than taxi cab drivers (13,587).[16] So, the answer to my question? Just shy of half a million people would lose their jobs.

I read a lot about taxi cab drivers feeling squeezed by rideshare providers like Uber and Lyft. Another threat, much less discussed by drivers, is autonomous vehicles. In the 19th century, the horse and buggy operators were replaced by the introduction of automobiles. I was beginning to feel a lot like the 19th Century horse and buggy. It was only a matter of time before taxi drivers and rideshare drivers were replaced by autonomous vehicles. Rideshare drivers should be the least of taxi cab drivers' worries.

Shane

I started my day at 6:30 am since the girls had a day off of school. I wanted to get a better idea of what the pay might look like at the heart of morning rush hour.

On arriving at the Westin Hotel, I saw a young man, Shane, who looked like he was leaving for his first day of college. I looked at the

---

[15] https://www.theverge.com/2017/11/8/16626224/las-vegas-self-driving-shuttle-crash-accident-first-day

[16] https://rideshareapps.com/2015-rideshare-infographic/

app to see where Shane was headed: Microsoft. I thought, they are grabbing them young these days.

As soon as he got into the car, I could tell Shane was nervous. He placed a large bag on the floor and started sorting, an effort which took the entire ride. I felt sorry for him, a fish out of water, his head buried in the bag.

The address he entered took us to Building 92 on the Microsoft Campus. It was the wrong address. Shane wanted to go to Building 111. Parked at Building 92, Shane got out of the car and said, "I should be able to find it from here."

It was raining. I could tell he was confused. I asked him, "Are you sure you don't want me to wait? Microsoft is a large campus."

Shane hesitated, but said, "No, I will be okay, but thanks."

I persisted one last time. "Look, if you give me a moment, I will look on my phone and see if I can locate Building 111."

Shane awkwardly nodded.

I told him, "I'll use Google maps to find the building, but sometimes Google maps is not accurate. I actually wonder sometimes if it is just an error on Google's part or a prank played on Microsoft by Google map developers."

James laughed.

I found the building on my app and James got back into the car. A short two minutes later, I was driving up to Building 111. Ahhhh... I thought. Now I know why Shane is so nervous. Building 111 is Microsoft's recruiting offices. Microsoft probably put him up at one of Bellevue's top hotels and is paying for the Uber. Shane is about to be interviewed by Microsoft.

I pulled up to Building 92 and said, "Here you go, Shane, Building 111. Have a great day!"

Shane said, "Thanks!" and got out of the car. I wanted to wish him well. I wanted to tell him that with his earnest approach, he was a shoo-in for the job. But I could tell James was close to an anxiety attack. I had no doubt James would do great. If James got this far in the process, he would most likely make it the rest of the way on his own.

Lauren, Crystal and Spencer

My next three fares came quickly. I picked up Lauren at the exclusive Bellevue Club Hotel. Lauren was headed to Redmond Town Center. As she got into the car, she was talking on her phone. When she sat down, she tapped her speaker button. The conference call she was on was no longer muted. For most of the fifteen-minute ride, I listened in on a terribly boring meeting. Wow, I thought, I do not miss meetings.

I dropped Lauren off at a Starbucks, thinking my interesting person of the day would be Shane. When I picked up Crystal, that changed. I ended up behaving like it was my first interview.

Crystal was sight-impaired. As I drove up, she was standing at the curb, looking up to the sky, and holding a red and white folding cane. I overreacted. I jumped out of the car to get her door and she was inside before I could even turn the corner. When I got back into my car, I reached over to move the passenger seat up so she could have more leg room. She let me know she was fine.

I was the person that obviously was not fine, so I focused my attention on what I should have been doing in the first place, driving her to the Microsoft Campus. Crystal took out what looked like a digital recorder and began to play something that sounded like another meeting, but on fast forward. I tried to listen but I could not make out what was being said. Back to driving.

When I drove up to the building, I double-parked as two cars were blocking the front door. I got out of the car and navigated Crystal into the front door of the building. Success! I believe I did one thing correctly.

I didn't have long to dwell on my lack of grace with Crystal, as I had another fare almost immediately. It would be my last of the day.

Spencer

Spencer, waiting in front of his house, was the first passenger I had who was an employee at Facebook. I was not shy about my ignorance. I said, "I didn't know Facebook was in Seattle."

"We're right off Dexter," he said. "Facebook has about 2000 employees in Seattle. They are leasing another two buildings so Facebook is expanding here."

I looked at my app and saw that I was not taking Spencer to Seattle. I was confused. "Are you going to work now?"

"Yes," he said. "I am going to catch the Facebook shuttle to Seattle."

The drive took five minutes and before I knew it, I dropped Spencer off where a Facebook shuttle was waiting. I couldn't help but marvel at all of the job opportunities in Seattle. I decided to call it a day as I had a hunch that my four successive trips would amount to my highest hourly wage to date.

I was right. I made eighteen dollars and eighty-six cents an hour. It would be interesting to see, outside of surge funding, if I ever make anything more than eighteen dollars and eighty-six cents an hour. It was the first time I had made an hourly rate higher than Seattle's minimum wage.

It was a good day. I broke the minimum wage barrier, and I was able to provide help to a young man going to a very important interview. I gave myself a small pat on the back. Come on, I thought, could a self-driving car provide such a high level of service? It was a small pat. There was no doubt about it. I was still a 21st Century horse and buggy driver. Change was inevitable.

VETERAN'S DAY BUST: THE DAY UBER COST ME
November 10, 2017, Friday

Trips	Time on Road	Miles	Uber Earnings	Vehicle Cost	Real Earnings	Hourly Wage
1	1 hr 53 min	66	$21.47	-$33.00	-$11.53	-$6.12

As soon as I launched my Uber app, I saw that I earned a new badge, "Expert Navigation". Thank you, Spencer, Microsoft recruit!

Uber identified some advanced surge pricing in Seattle from 7 am to 9 am. I decided to go to Seattle to see what it might be like to participate in surge pricing. Based on yesterday's high hourly wage, I wanted to see if I could set a new record on the hourly wage front.

I set my destination to Seattle, but had no takers, so off I went over the bridge, sans passengers. In just less than twelve minutes, I arrived at Seattle (6:59 am) ready to reap the surge pricing pot of gold. At 7:15 am, still no passengers. Maybe I was on the low end of Uber's queue? Maybe there were too many drivers on the road? I went on Uber's passenger app and up popped a fleet of Uber cars either in transit or, like myself, waiting for passengers.

I pulled over in a no parking zone. The sign, right in front me, read, "No Parking". I waited another fifteen minutes in the no parking zone and still no calls for rides. So off I went to avoid the possibility of a costly fine. I would return to Bellevue. As I arrived in Bellevue, I had a fare.

Beth

Although the trip was booked under the name Mark, it was actually for Mark's wife, Beth. Beth would later tell me, "I don't know a lot about technology. My husband had to get me the cab on his phone."

Beth ran out of the house, her husband nipping at her heels. A quick peck on her cheek and Beth was inside the car. Beth was absolutely delightful.

One of Beth's girlfriends was having a birthday party, and she was super pumped to be on her way to a girl's weekend in Minneapolis. Beth didn't have any checked bags, and she did not have to check in any children. Beth was free.

Beth's enthusiasm was so contagious, I became excited. Looking around, Beth noticed beauty everywhere. When we passed fog rolling in around Lake Washington, she exclaimed, "Look at how beautiful the fog is!" It was as if she was given a new lease on life and her eyes were open for the first time in a very long time.

Beth talked and I listened. I didn't hear everything she said as I became lost in the sound of her unabashed happiness. Even when she asked a question, I knew it was more for herself than me, "I'm going to my girlfriend's new home that is absolutely beautiful. It cost $350,000. What kind of home can you buy for $350,000 in Bellevue?"

At some point, Beth heard herself ramble on and abruptly stopped. "I'm sorry for carrying on like this," she said. "I'm just so excited to be going on a trip. How has it been driving for Uber?"

I provided Beth with a brief overview of Uber. She listened just as eagerly, expressing surprise that nearly 500,000 drivers could eventually lose their jobs to self-driving cars. Beth was not only passionate, but compassionate. I was curious, so I asked Beth, "How much do you think an Uber driver makes hourly?"

Beth answered, "I would think they earn somewhere between $15 and $20 per hour."

Beth was astonished when I gave her my estimate of $10 to $15 per hour. "How can anyone support themselves on that?" she asked sadly.

With Beth in the car, I lost track of time, and before I knew it, we arrived at the airport. I pulled over and got Beth's bag. Beth took the bag and literally skipped from my car to inside the terminal. Okay, maybe I just imagined that as I could have just as easily seen her floating to her connection.

I was pumped both by the ride and the knowledge that I earned at least a few dollars for the day. But I calmed down, since the more I thought about it, the more I realized I most probably operated at a loss. On my drive back from Seattle, I took the toll bridge which cost me an additional four dollars and thirty cents out of pocket. If I subtract the toll cost from the twenty-five dollars and seventy cents I made for the trip to the airport, my Uber Earnings were only twenty-one dollars and forty-seven cents. I returned to reality. Things were looking bad, at least on the fiscal side.

I needed to pick up my wife at the train station, so I set my destination to the Everett Amtrak station. If I picked up a passenger on the way to the train station, who knew, maybe I could break even. No such luck. Once again, I concluded my trip empty-handed.

I started the day, hoping to break my hourly record by travelling to a region identified by Uber in advance as surge pricing. I came back with a record, but instead of a record high, achieved a record low. I was out of pocket eleven dollars and fifty-three cents and my hourly earnings was a negative six dollars and twelve cents per hour. That hurt.

I miscalculated badly on my attempt to strike boldly in surge rich Seattle. Today's loss was an error on my part as it most probably occurred due to the Veteran's Day holiday. But why did Uber advertise surge pricing? I chalked the loss to another learning experience: be wary of Uber's published surge rates and anticipate slower traffic on some holidays.

Fortunately, I had the luxury to pay for the learning experience. Most did not. Still, not a great day. But in my heart of hearts, I knew, at the very least, that somewhere in Minnesota, Beth was having enough fun for the two of us.

CHAPTER SEVEN

TIPS

ARE YOU KIDDING ME
November 11, 2017, Saturday

I glanced down at the Uber home screen and saw I was eligible for tips. What? I wondered, how long has that been there? Why now? I would learn later that while the tipping option was reported broadly, tipping was only gradually phased in and had only recently been introduced into the Seattle market.

I turned my attention to the app. It appeared I only had to press the button which I did. I didn't get a response so I assumed the tipping mechanism was now active for all my passengers. I would have to wait and see.

For just over a month, it wasn't even possible for passengers to tip on the app and Uber never said a word. All this time, I had in the back of my mind been blaming myself, thinking it was something I did. Ughhhhh! No wonder drivers were using tip jars in their car.

None of this should have been unexpected from this faceless boss. I only had myself to blame. Communication was a one way street. Uber was more Big Brother than partner. I was slowly waking up to some new realities. But at the very least, I was waking up.

EMPTY-HANDED
November 12, 2017, Sunday

The weekend was here, so I reviewed my total revenue for the past five days: one hundred and forty-two dollars and fifty-two cents. If it were not for my experience with the passengers, the news would be depressing. Then the thought hit me: Why not try driving again on a Sunday afternoon, a sort *Driving Miss Daisy*. I had a decent experience with a Sunday afternoon once before and maybe the extra one or two hours would carry me over my weekly goal of two hundred dollars. Still bothered by the low weekly earnings, I decided it was worth a try.

As I did not get good phone reception in my parking garage, I drove out of the garage and searched for curbside parking in my neighborhood. Once I found parking, I would read and/or write in the car while waiting for a fare. Passenger or not, it was a win/win situation, or so I thought.

I was reminded quickly that finding a parking spot in Bellevue is a lot like winning the lottery. And on Sunday afternoon, after driving several blocks, I came up empty. I should have known better. Bellevue had become one of the fastest growing cities in the United States, with a population of more than 141,000 residents.

I had not given up hope when an idea flashed through my mind. Bellevue recently opened its downtown park and it was a good bet there would be plenty of parking in their new parking lot. SCORE! Not only did I have an easy spot to pull into, but I had a beautiful view of the park.

When I turned on my app, I saw on the home page an announcement that the tipping function was now active. I now had some incentive to wait, so I decided to wait thirty minutes for a call. I turned off my car, raised the volume on my phone so as to alert me of any incoming passenger calls, and opened *Tales of the Fairies and the Ghost World* by Jeremiah Curtin. Thirty minutes went by. No calls.

That did it. I was done for the day. I turned on my car and drove home, empty-handed. I was disappointed and it wasn't because of the money. I turned into that person you meet at a cocktail party who is always looking for the next person to talk to. In this situation, I'm just looking for that next person to drive. Unfortunately, no one showed up to this Uber party. On top of that, tips were dangled in front of me making the party even more attractive. For all intents and purposes, Uber stood me up.

SEATTLE TIMES
November 13, 2017, Monday

Trips	Time on Road	Miles	Uber Earnings	Vehicle Cost	Real Earnings	Hourly Wage
6	2 hr 50 min	76	$81.73	-$38.00	$48.03	$15.43

After Sunday's experience, I wanted a new start. I bought a *Seattle Times* and placed it in the back of my car. I wanted to see if the presence of a daily paper added any value to the passenger's experience. So, each time a passenger entered the car, I welcomed them, letting them know the newspaper was available for their use. I then let them know if they wanted the temperature in the car adjusted, to just let me know.

Incredibly, not one of my six passengers picked up the newspaper. Worse, when I picked up my first UberPool passengers (UberPool is an Uber service for passengers heading in the same direction that opt to ride with each other), the newspaper became an inconvenience, taking up needed space. It would become the first and last day I made a newspaper available for passengers.

Tips

While the newspaper was a failure, my day was not. I set multiple records: I had the most passengers, the longest time on the clock (two hours and fifty minutes), and the farthest distance traveled (seventy-six miles). My first drive took me to the Microsoft campus in Redmond, my second drive took me through heavy traffic to the Amazon campus in Seattle, and once in Seattle, I experienced my first UberPool drive, in the University of Washington district. Leaving Seattle, I completed my longest one-way drive. And, maybe more importantly, I received that elusive first tip.

That one tip was a confidence builder. The tip felt like an additional badge, another way to compliment the driver. And given the hourly wage, a possible way to make Uber more doable as a part-time occupation. As far as Uber being a full-time endeavor, I needed a lot more convincing.

Kerri

The tip[17] came from my first passenger, Kerri, who I picked up at the Residence Inn in Bellevue. Kerri entered the car, greeted me, and proceeded to spend the rest of the car ride putting on her make-up. Given how many people I drive to work, I expected to see more people putting on make-up in the car. Maybe putting make-up in front of a stranger has become a social faux pas? I doubt it. Regardless, I wish I had the chance to thank Kerri for that two dollars and forty cents tip.

Vince

Once I dropped Kerri off at Microsoft, I was on my way to pick up Vince in Kirkland. Vince, like Roberto, had a strong presence and projected both strength and optimism. As soon as he got into the car, and for only the second time, Vince asked me how my day was going. It happened so rarely, I was caught off guard.

I said, "Great. Thanks for asking. How is your day going?"

Vince said, "Great. I am fairly new in town. I am actually heading to the Amazon campus. I just started a job there."

"What do you do at Amazon?"

"I work in Amazon's web services in the energy commodities department."

"Energy commodities department at Amazon?" I said slowly. "I didn't know Amazon had that kind of depth. How did you get into that area?"

"I spent six years with Merrill Lynch, trading energy commodities in Chicago before relocating to Vancouver, Canada. I just moved to Kirkland from Vancouver so I am still getting to know the area and the job."

---

[17]The driver's App clearly identifies when a trip includes a tip. As some people don't tip right away, I usually checked my app at the end of the day, to see if, and then who tipped.

"How do you like working at Amazon?" I asked.

"Well," Vince reflected. "It's not an easy place to work, but fortunately, I am on the right team. The biggest challenge is that most of my colleagues have graduate degrees. I am actually thinking about doing my graduate degree."

"That's a great idea. Where are you thinking of going?"

"Wharton, but the $215,000 price tag is intimidating."

"I imagine an Ivy league education comes with a lot of financial benefits. I am sure you've done your own cost-benefit analysis. Will you make your money back?"

Vince laughed. I imagine he didn't expect to be having this level of conversation with his Uber driver. "I actually did a cost-benefit analysis," he acknowledged. "And the jury is out. My experience has put me where I am today. I just can't see how much farther I can go with a graduate degree, no matter where it is from."

"Does family weigh into your decision?" I asked.

"That is my other challenge," Vince confessed. "I probably need to figure out my personal life first. My girlfriend is a native of Vancouver. She is getting ready to join me in Kirkland. We've talked a lot about the beauty of the northwest and I would really like to make a home in Seattle. But until she gets here, I can't really bank on her joining me."

"I like your conservative approach," I said as we pulled up to his building on the Amazon campus. "As I see it, you are an articulate and intelligent person with an incredible future ahead of you. I imagine she will be joining you very soon."

Vince smiled. The drive took just over thirty minutes, and given the animated conversation, it felt like five minutes. It felt good to be back behind the wheel and once again, I was enjoying Seattle.

UberPool

When I dropped Vince off, I experienced my first UberPool, the option that allows the rider to get a lower fare if they are willing to share the ride with other riders. It is very popular with budget conscious university students. Until today, I did not even know my car was eligible for UberPool.

Artyom

Artyom, a student at the University of Washington, was my first passenger and fortunately, he was more than happy to explain how UberPool worked. Since I was unfamiliar with UberPool, I was worried I would not get Artyom to his destination as I was being directed by the app toward another UberPool passenger. In this situation, we exchanged roles. Artyom had to calm me down.

Just before I stopped to pick up the next UberPool passenger, Kilee, I thanked Artyom for explaining to me how UberPool worked. After I picked up Kilee, I did not hear another word from Artyom or Kilee. Until we reached Artyom's destination, an awkward silence descended on the car. It appeared there was no protocol on conversation between pool passengers. I waited to see how long the uncomfortable silence would proceed. Yep. All the way until I dropped Artyom off.

I dropped off Kilee at the UW Campus, made a quick three-minute drive for another UW student and then thought about returning home. That was a lot of excitement for one day. But before I could leave Seattle, I was tagged for another fare.

Mei

I pulled into a gas station and opened the door for Mei. Mei was beautiful. I looked at her once and decided not to look again, just in case I stared.

When I got into the front seat and closed the door, I breathed in a heady fragrance of perfume. Mei, at 11 am in the morning, was dressed like it was a weekend night. I let her know about the newspaper and asked her whether she would like the temperature in the car changed, only to discover she had limited English. When I looked at her destination, I did a double take – Maryville, 31.79 miles away and about a 40-minute drive. Yikes. I checked her destination, again, another double take... Tulalip Resort Casino.

Given the destination was the Casino, I really wanted to know Mei's story. But given the communication barrier, I drove in silence. My mind wandered. Was she a dancer? An escort? Aghhhhhh! None of my business. Letting her off at the front door of the Casino, I called it a day and made the long journey back.

The tip was certainly the highlight of my day. For months, I thought the tipping option was already in place. I had no idea Uber was phasing in tipping and it had only just arrived in Seattle. But when I saw a two dollar and forty cents tip included in my total revenue at the end of the day, I was ecstatic. How awesome is that? I might have just as well gotten a hundred dollars. Did I feel bad that only one out of six fares left a tip? Not at all. I had been trained not to expect tips. Uber passengers have been trained not to tip.

Before going home, I decided to go to the DMV. I had two more tasks to accomplish before I could drive for Lyft. Uber never mailed me back my registration so I was not able to upload it on the Lyft app. At the DMV, I waited one hour, paid ten dollars, and in two minutes, the woman assisting me printed off my registration. I took a picture of the registration and promptly uploaded it to my Lyft application. All I had to do was have my vehicle inspection and I would be ready to drive for Lyft.

MERCER ISLAND AND BELLEVUE'S EASTGATE
November 14, 2017, Tuesday

Trips	Time on Road	Miles	Uber Earnings	Vehicle Cost	Real Earnings	Hourly Wage
2	1 hr 1 min	21	$26.16	-$10.50	$15.66	$15.40

I woke up with the flu, stepped into the shower, and then made an emergency run to the bathroom where I spent several minutes looking into a porcelain bowl, reflecting on what illness does to people needing part-time or full-time income. The bottom line in the rideshare business: if you're ill and you don't go to work, you don't get paid. Sick leave, another benefit I was used to my entire career, was something I obviously took for granted. Drivers didn't have it.

People driving on a part time basis are using the income as discretionary dollars to offset rent, make a car payment, pay school bills or to just have the money to go out to dinner or see a show. For people driving full time, wages are used to pay a mortgage/rent, buy food, pay bills, etc. I imagine any type of lengthy illness could be devastating to either person if they are relying on the income to pay any sort of monthly bills.

I decided to buck up and not let a little illness stop me. If I could drive my daughters to their bus stop, I could certainly continue to Uber. As I pulled in to my daughters' bus stop, I looked down at my Uber map. The Bellevue area turned dark orange and dark red, almost like a storm. Surge pricing was in effect.

I got the girls' attention and pointed to the Uber storm brewing on the map. The girls became excited and ran out of the car to their bus stop so I could take advantage of the surge pricing. Lo and behold, I picked up a passenger with surge pricing. My daughters were going to be thrilled.

Nirmaai

I picked up my surge passenger, Nirmaai, at the Sheraton and discovered, pretty quickly, a language barrier. No matter, I was delighted at the thought of surge pricing and was looking forward to finding out the difference surge pricing would make on the fare.

I drove Nirmaai to Siemens in Bellevue's Eastgate. Siemens, Europe's largest manufacturing company, had an office in Bellevue which was responsible for digital manufacturing. I was somewhat familiar with Siemens as it sat in Bellevue College's backyard, Washington state's largest two-year college.

Traffic was a mess, what with students headed off to college, and employees on their way to work. The congestion on the roads was much worse than my typical drives either to the Microsoft campus or to the Amazon campus. The five-mile slog through traffic took sixteen minutes to complete. On the plus side, surge pricing added just under ten dollars to the fare. Julia and Emma would be delighted. I was.

Jose

The surge fare left me a little pumped, so I decided to press on and pick up Jose in Mercer Island. Although Mercer Island was an arm's throw from Bellevue, it was the first time I picked up anyone from that area. Mercer Island, a city on an island that bears the same name, connects Bellevue and Seattle across a floating bridge on I-90. I love driving through Mercer Island, so I was looking forward to picking up Jose.

As soon as Jose got into the car, he started to give me directions, somewhat anxiously. I turned around and told him, "Hey, please wait. If you give me a moment, I will turn down the volume on my Uber app. This way, I will ignore Uber and just rely on your directions."

Jose looked perplexed, then relieved, as it took a few moments for Jose to understand that I was actually listening to him. "You know," he confessed, "yesterday, I took an Uber and the driver did not want to take directions from me."

"Well," I said reassuringly, "you are in the right. I was reading some of Uber's literature on their website. Drivers are actively encouraged to take directions from the passengers. And as you are the passenger, by all means, lead the way."

Jose went from being anxious to being my best friend. Between giving me directions, Jose started to talk to me about himself, "I am on my way to work at Booking.com."

"What do you do?"

"I am a Spanish and English tech."

An eager audience, I asked: "Where did you learn Spanish?"

"I was born in Venezuela and have only been in the US a few months. I love this country."

I had been reading about the crises in Venezuela. Once oil prices dropped, the country was thrown into economic chaos. The United States, in the midst of a wave of anti-immigrant mania, was apparently opening its arms to one country in particular, refugees from Venezuela. Whether Jose was here seeking asylum or here for work or both, he didn't disclose.

After Jose provided me a short history on the current leadership crises in Venezuela, I asked him, "How has your transition been to the United States?"

"Not too bad. I have been using Uber to travel back and forth to work because I haven't been able to buy a car. Yesterday, Ford financing turned me down. The Ford dealership wanted to see assets of fifty thousand dollars because of my residency status."

Jose was pretty worked up about the experience, so I didn't question him further. Sometimes I tried to be helpful, other times I tried to be empathetic. I just listened and periodically groaned with him. By the time we reached Booking.com, the conversation was only picking up steam.

Jose was pretty frustrated by his car situation. I thought about asking Jose if he wanted to continue the conversation later. Again, I reminded myself, Uber driver. With no prompting, Jose thanked me for the drive, got out of the car, and started walking toward his building.

I found out later that Jose left me a gift, one dollar. The tip was the most rewarding dollar I ever earned. It might as well have been a hundred dollars.

Even though I was under the weather, the day was a good one. In just over a month of driving, I never made a trip to Bellevue's Eastgate. Now, in one day, I made two trips to Eastgate. And although I only worked one hour, it came out to another fifteen dollars plus an hour. Slow, but steady progress.

CHAPTER EIGHT

DIVORCE

MAKING ENDS MEET
November 15, 2017, Wednesday

Trips	Time on Road	Miles	Uber Earnings	Vehicle Cost	Real Earnings	Hourly Wage
5	3 hr 53 min	102	$88.88	-$51.00	$37.88	$9.75

We were living in a boom economy and then, to my utter amazement, I read the headline: "Pay raises: Survey indicated 52% of workers didn't get one in the past year."[18] Yikes! More than half of Americans did not get a pay raise? How could that be?

It was no wonder rideshare careers in companies like Uber were skyrocketing. In a time of inflation, people needed to make up lost income, one way or the other. Did Uber drivers see an increase in their earnings over the past year? Somehow, even with the tip option, I didn't think so. And for many on the West Coast, making a living was more difficult than ever.

Last night over dinner with a couple of friends, I learned it took a family income of seventy-two thousand dollars a year to live in

---

[18] https://www.usatoday.com/story/money/careers/changing-jobs/2017/11/15/pay-raises-survey-indicates-52-workers-didnt-get-one-past-year/864433001/

Bellevue.[19] Double yikes! If I got a tip now, I better be double grateful. It appeared that even in good times, the majority of people still faced rough times.

Having stayed out late the evening before, I decided to see what it would be like to work a late afternoon shift. The later shift meant I had time to get a haircut and a shave, from my own personal confessor and barber, Mario. Getting a shave from Mario was like stepping back into a 19th century Italian hair salon. Mario had a strong family history in this most ancient profession. Mario's grandfather was a barber in Florence, Italy, before migrating to the United States in 1928.

Mario worked at *Bellevue's House of Styles*, a barbershop dedicated to perfecting the classic shave and haircut. I was pretty sure Mario did it for effect, but he sported an impeccably groomed handlebar mustache. His long mustache curved upward at the ends, reminding me of the wild west figure, Wyatt Earp.

Almost as soon as I sat into the barber's chair, I started to update Mario, with whom I shared previously that I was writing a book on my Uber experience. "I am telling you Mario, the stories I'm hearing from passengers are so interesting. It is amazing to me how much people will share with a complete stranger."

Mario laughed. "Are you kidding me? You can't imagine what people share with me, sitting in this chair." Mario spun my chair around for emphasis. "Just last week, I was doing the hair of a young lady who was driving for Lyft."

I sat back in my chair and relaxed. I should have known better. Every time I got my haircut, Mario was a warehouse of stories. But this time, before he could tell me his story, I had to tell him of my connection to Lyft. "That's a coincidence. Even though I am driving for Uber, I am getting my vehicle inspected tomorrow by Lyft. I am going to compare Lyft with Uber."

"Well," Mario said, "the young lady, I am sad to say, was filthy. Her hair was dirty and the only thing I could think about was what her car must look like."

---

[19] My friends source was Hopelink, an area agency that helps the poor.

"You know, Mario, I don't believe that either Uber or Lyft have a dress code."

The bottom line was that as independent contractors, drivers could pretty much wear whatever they waned. I recalled two quotes by drivers in my research that emphasized this thought dramatically.

> *Driver One*
> "I find the raggiest clothes with holes in them to wear. My shoes have duct tape around them. My hat is older than me. There is no sense of putting out money for clothes that you don't have."[20]
>
> *Driver Two*
> "Salvation Army has all of your clothing needs. I used to get new shirts for a quarter!"[21]

Not to be outdone by Mario, I said, "I think you would be surprised by the interesting people I have met while driving."

Being the consummate barber, Mario said, "Barbers and drivers meet interesting people every day. Barbers are a lot like Uber drivers."

Not wanting to correct a man with a razor at my throat, I decided to throw caution to the wind and set him straight.

"Two things," I said. "First, to do your job, Mario, you have to have skills. To drive for Uber, all you need is a pulse, a driver's license, insurance, a criminal background check, and a car; no skills required. They don't even know if you are a good driver or not. Second, in your business, you have a lot of repeat business. Look at me, I am here every month, getting a haircut and a shave from you, so I know you do a lot of repeat business. On the other hand, I've been driving for Uber for five weeks and I have not had one repeat customer. People talk to you, but they know they have the opportunity to continue the conversation at their next haircut. I am one ride and gone. I am a one-nighter for passengers. Sometimes, I get an entire life story squeezed into ten minutes."

---

[20] https://uberpeople.net/threads/uber-dress-code.150844/

[21] Ibid.

We laughed as we compared the venerable and time-honored position of barber to the gig Uber driver. By the end of my shave, I was no match for Mario and Mario knew it. Where I treated Uber as a self-indulgent escapade, Mario turned barbering into a lifestyle.

"Maybe I should write a book on my customers," Mario said with a devilish smile.

Haircut and shave completed, my soul once again wiped clean by my barber, I was ready to get back on the road, or was I? Still ill from the day before, I had second thoughts about going out. Like many people, I start with a lot of energy in the morning, but begin to fade in the late afternoon. I should have trusted my instincts.

Ouch, what traffic. And, it seemed like each ride I took, I kept going farther and farther south until I wound up just over an hour away from home. Sick, but well groomed, I put in my longest day to date in rush hour traffic, almost four hours in bumper to bumper traffic. As I have spoken with drivers that put in twelve-hour days on a regular basis, I have no reason to complain. I was coming to enjoy driving as a hobby, but making a living?

Cindy

At the start of rush hour, I picked up Cindy at Hermes, one of the Shops at Bravern, Bellevue's high-end shopping center where "one can find the world's ultimate luxury brands." Cindy entered sans bags, but appeared to have enjoyed her walk through Bellevue's most fashionable stores. In five minutes, I had her safely home at an apartment complex behind Bellevue's Main Street.

Rob

I returned to the Shops at Bravern and picked up Rob at the John Howe Steak House. Rob, an older, well-dressed man, had, unlike Cindy, engaged in some heavy-duty shopping and was carrying several brightly colored shopping bags. Rob was standing on the sidewalk speaking intimately with a young, and equally well-dressed Filipino man. Boyfriend?

The young man gave me some nasty stares. Wow, I thought, I hoped he wouldn't be joining Rob. The young man was certainly flamboyant. When the young man departed, he literally swaggered in front of my car, giving me what looked like the evil eye. Was I perceived as competition? It was a little unnerving. I was relieved he didn't get into the car.

Rob was a salesman and from the looks of things, a very successful salesman. He flew into Seattle from Missoula, Montana and was heading out to Las Vegas. He had just gotten off a three-hour conference call with China, and as soon as he got into the car, proceeded to another conference call.

Once again, the conference call was placed on his speaker phone, so I guess, in a way, I also attended the conference. I turned off the radio and kept my mouth shut. Rob appeared to be leading the meeting.

Rob described an area in China as a market opportunity for a new medical technology that tested for cancer in patients with oral health care issues. The pharmaceutical scientists that developed the test had no idea how to monetize certain markets. That was where Rob came in and he seized the opportunity.

Rob knew China was a perfect place to introduce the cancer assessment as China allowed greater flexibility in introducing new products. With 95 million people living in the targeted area, the market was a huge opportunity. Rob was excited. Listening in on the conference call was like attending a short course on entrepreneurship.

When we arrived at the airport, Rob brought his meeting to a close. He thanked me for the ride, got back on his cell phone, and headed off to his terminal. Getting Rob to the airport took a little over thirty minutes in heavy traffic, but I enjoyed every moment of the conference call.

The return traffic looked bad, but the conference call itself was worth the trip. I decided I might as well find another rider in the area and attempt, if possible, to wait out rush hour. I was surprised to find a passenger quickly. As luck would have it, the passenger was near the airport.

Mark

I picked up Mark who lived in Spring Trees Condominiums, or what is a nice way of saying a trailer park. Mark had been sitting at home all day, alone, busting at the bit to get out and have a conversation with anyone. Mark spent the next eleven minutes telling me all about himself.

"I need to get to the shop in downtown Renton to pick up my car," he said.

"Everything okay?" I asked.

"The lights on my car stopped working so I have the car at the shop to get them fixed. I've been without a car for two days."

"What kind of car?"

"It's a 2001 Ford Focus."

"That's incredible! I am pretty sure they started to make the Focus about that time. Do you know what year the first Focus was made?"

"1999."

"Wow! "

"Yeah, my Focus is the first and the only car I have ever owned."

"That's pretty surprising. There has to be a lot of stories behind that car."

Mark laughed. Mark kept the car because it was practical to do so. I don't believe his life went "according to plan". Mark was currently unemployed. He spent six years in Wisconsin, near Green Bay, where he ran a political campaign and was a manager of an ice cream store, two very different jobs. He was studying for his LSAT's in the hopes of becoming a lawyer. He asked me a lot of intelligent questions, reminding me of Student Government presidents I used to work with. But Mark had to be at least thirty-five years old, so I wasn't sure what led him to this point in his life, living in a trailer park, still maintaining his 2001 Ford Focus.

I enjoyed listening to Mark, but the ride was coming to an end. If I was my barber, Mario, I would have had the opportunity to look forward to hearing more. I really wanted to know how an obviously intelligent guy like Mark found himself unemployed, living in Spring Hills Condominiums, and still in possession of his first car.

When we arrived at the shop, Mark surprised me and said, "Maybe I should try driving for Uber."

"Mark," I said, "Uber would be a great job for you as part-time income. You are friendly and have an easy-going manner and obviously enjoy talking with people. Unfortunately, Uber requires the car to be a four door and I am pretty sure your car is a two door."

"Yeah," Mark replied with a little bit of dejection in his voice. He reached over, shook my hand, and said, "But I sure enjoyed the ride."

"Me, too," I said. Mark was an extremely likeable fellow. What brought him to Spring Hills Condominium was a mystery. I wished I could take him under my wing, let him use my car to do a few Uber rides. But nowhere on the app was there an "extra support button". And who knew what Mark was really like? His stories certainly did not match up to his reality.

Anthony

Fortunately, late afternoon seemed to be a hopping time to be a driver. I had another fare as soon as I left the shop. I picked up Anthony, who, like Rob, needed to get to the airport. Anthony was quiet the entire ride and as I did not want to invade his peace, I remained quiet. I started to wonder how long it would take me to get home in such heavy traffic. Could I really get another fare at the airport? If I did get another fare, would it take me back to Bellevue or take me even farther away from home?

Bam, another fare popped up. But it was an UberPool, and I really wanted to get home, so I declined. As soon as I cancelled, another fare popped up and it was Uberx (the standard Uber service). I didn't know where the fare was going, but I was feeling lucky. Rush hour driving, maybe I could do this.

Tass and Abdel

I was not lucky. I drove to the Southcenter Mall in Tukwilla to find Tass. Tass was in the middle of the parking lot, speaking Arabic to his friend, Abdel. The ride was for Abdel.

When I looked at the destination, I saw I was headed to Tacoma, a one hour drive even farther south in rush hour traffic. Abdel stepped into the car and asked, "Do you have a phone charger?"

Without saying a word, I disconnected my phone from my charger and handed it to him.

Still making my way out of the mall parking lot, Abdel, in a panicked voice, made his second request, "Stop the car."

A little startled, I did not panic. I pulled over next to a line of parked cars. I turned around and faced Abdel, saying, "Is there anything wrong?"

"I left my iPad with Tass. Can you please wait? My friend will come and give me my iPad."

"Not a problem. Let me pull into a parking spot and we will wait."

We waited another five minutes until Tass walked across the parking lot to return Abdel's iPad. This trip was getting worse and worse.

For the next almost thirty miles, which took one hour and one minute, Abdel did not say a word. Language barrier? I wasn't sure.

Even driving in a carpool lane, we moved slowly. When we finally got off the highway, we took a route to some obscure location in Tacoma's netherland. It was beginning to feel like a scene out of the *Blair Witch Project*.

Driving in silence, I reflected I at least had the satisfaction of setting a number of new records. I now reached the most miles in a day, the most revenue in a day, and the most time worked in a day (about four hours). But really, all I could think about was the additional one hour plus drive it would take to get back home, most probably without a passenger.

We finally arrived at our destination, a remote, dingy-looking gas station. No one appeared to waiting for Abdel. I became a little uncomfortable leaving Abdel at such a secluded location. I asked Abdel, "Are you going to be okay here?"

"Yes," he said and proceeded to return my charger. Just when Abdel was about to get out of the car, he turned to me and said, "Would you like to go in and get a tea or coffee? My treat."

I was a little taken back by the unexpected kindness, but as I was now a little tired and maybe a little cranky at being stranded so far from home, I thanked him for his offer and said I should be on my way home. I regretted my decision almost immediately. Abdel probably had an interesting story to tell.

The return trip took a little less than an hour. I kept my app on with my destination set to Bellevue, but there were no fares to be found. Waiting was not unusual for drivers. I met many drivers that waited an hour before getting a fare. I don't know how they do it.

That day, because of that long drive back with no passenger, I made nine dollars and seventy-five cents an hour. Not even a decent part-time wage. But maybe there was hope at the end of the rainbow. My vehicle inspection for Lyft was the next day. Once I completed the vehicle inspection and started driving for Lyft, I could find out whether my hourly wage increased. Again, one could only hope.

MY NEW BEST FRIEND
November 16, 2017, Thursday

Trips	Time on Road	Miles	Uber Earnings	Vehicle Cost	Real Earnings	Hourly Wage
1	30 min	9	$15.16	-$4.50	$10.66	$21.32

Even though my Lyft vehicle inspection was scheduled for 12 pm, I decided I would squeeze in an Uber drive. I could see, as I was driving the girls to their bus stop, that surge pricing was back. My one ride was uneventful, but the result was my highest hourly wage.

I picked up my passenger at the Sheraton in Bellevue and drove him in short order to his destination on the Microsoft Campus. During the short ride, he prepared himself for whatever business he was conducting with Microsoft, while I enjoyed the anticipation of finding out what the surge fare rate would mean to my hourly rate after yesterday's dismal performance. When I completed the ride, I looked down at my app and saw that the surge fare was six dollars and twenty-four cents. I was delighted by the amount. I reached a new high on the hourly wage front: twenty-one dollars and thirty-two cents.

I turned off my Uber app and made my way to the Lyft vehicle inspection in Seattle. I have to admit, I was a little pumped. Earlier, I received a letter for a Lyft "Driver Welcome Meeting" and the meeting included dinner. The invite was nice, given my experience with Uber. What a great way to welcome new drivers.

Lyft Inspection

Driving over to the Lyft inspection, my expectations remained low. Lyft is a smaller company than Uber, so I expected to find the same squalid surroundings as the Uber Hub. Wrong!

I paralleled parked on Western Avenue and walked into a clean and spacious office space. A well-dressed young man in a black two-piece suit greeted me at the door to check me in. He was, shall I say, unabashedly cheery. "Hello. How can I help you?"

I gave him my name. He smiled, and looked down at a piece of paper in front of him containing a list of names. This was not what I expected. The man was professional, the space was professional. I was starting to feel like I entered the Twilight Zone.

As the young man looked up my name, I glanced around the Lyft office. To my right was a coffee stand. Above the coffee stand were shelves of candy. The candies rested in large, glass, see-through jars. Each jar was filled with a different, brightly colored sweet with a large spoon placed in the middle like one might find in a candy store. Beyond the coffee stand was another service desk where three people sat, waiting to be of assistance.

The young man looked up from his paperwork and said, "Yes, Raymond. I have you right here."

Another young man, at the end of the service desk and listening to the conversation, spoke up and said, "Raymond, why don't you come over here and I will assist you."

Given my Uber Hub experience, I was in a state of shock. I walked numbly over to the second jolly young man. He handed me what looked like a gift package. It was a Lyft information kit. The package contained Lyft stickers and information I would need to drive.

The young man, I was too much in a daze to remember his name, went over a worksheet with me. He emphasized that I would need to acquire a Seattle business license, otherwise, I could be subject to a hundred dollar fine if I was pulled over in Seattle. Uber never even suggested a business license. After he finished going over the work sheet, he asked me if I had any questions. I numbly shook my head no.

He then said, "You are now ready for the vehicle inspection," and handed me a one-page vehicle checklist. Wow, I thought, this list is long. Finally, the real monster has surfaced. Lyft may have an inviting office with snacks and treats, a great presentation and orientation kit, and a more thorough vehicle checklist, but it looks like I will now be here forever, waiting for my car to be inspected.

I started to imagine long lines when the young man asked me again if I had any other questions. I was still reeling from the extraordinary hospitality to think of any questions. With a quiet nod of approval, (maybe he was used to drivers coming over from Uber to experience this elevated state of being), he gave me directions to the vehicle inspection, only a block up the street. As I was leaving, he handed me an additional pamphlet titled, "Tax tips for Lyft Drivers."

Walking out the door, I couldn't help but think, these people are the best.

Given my Uber experience, I was still waiting for the other shoe to fall. I had no doubt the bureaucracy would take over as I would meet some young person who would spend the next several hours checking off the numerous boxes on the one-page vehicle checklist. I was looking forward to it. Karma had to kick in, given the first-class treatment I was provided in the Lyft office.

I got into my car and drove a block and there it was, a nondescript indoor parking garage, which played directly into my low expectations. I pulled into the parking garage, followed the signs to "Lyft Inspection" and was met by not one, but three young men, neatly dressed, who immediately got out of their seats on seeing me.

The first young man greeted me and welcomed me to the inspection while the other two got to work on my car.

"Welcome," he said, "if you can step out of the car and wait over there, it will only take a few minutes."

A few minutes, hmmm. No way. I then moved, somewhat lamely, to where a solid, yet comfortable looking chair was waiting for me. I started to sit down when I began to watch a miracle at work.

The man that greeted me walked over and joined his two compadres, whereupon the three young men turned into a NASCAR pit team. I never sat down in the chair. I found myself standing back up as I watched them work on my car. I had become a driver at the Indianapolis 500.

I remained standing about three minutes when the man walked back over to me and said, "Congratulations, you have passed the vehicle inspection. I will upload the form and you will only have to wait two days until the background check is complete. Then you can begin driving."

I thanked him with that deer in the headlights look. Oh my God! I was falling in love with Lyft. I had went from Uber's *we don't care if you are alive or dead* to being treated like a professional by the courteous Lyft staff. When I got home, I received a text alert from Lyft: "Your application has been approved and you can start driving today." Icing on the cake.

A FAMILY AFFAIR
November 17, 2017, Friday

Trips	Time on Road	Miles	Uber Earnings	Vehicle Cost	Real Earnings	Hourly Wage
4	1 hr 31 min	31	$39.97	-$15.50	$24.47	$16.13

Lyft was drawing me into their family. I made a decision. As it was Friday, I would complete the week with one more Uber run. After that, the divorce would be complete and I would become a Lyft driver. This also fit into my travel plans.

I was going on Thanksgiving vacation for the next couple of weeks to Orlando, Florida. I would wait until I returned from vacation to start driving for Lyft. While on vacation, I would use Uber multiple times as a passenger. I would interview the drivers and see whether my experience lined up with their experiences.

When I returned from vacation, I would start with a clean slate. I would have documented both my experience as an Uber driver and my interviews with Uber drivers. I would be ready to begin my driving for Lyft. So today might very well be my last day driving for Uber.

Sean

Sean, waiting at the Red Lion, was upset. The shuttle was supposed to have arrived 45 minutes ago, and he was now late. His destination was Expedia, just a few blocks away. The Expedia building is a marquee building in Bellevue with the Expedia name proudly displayed on its roof. If Sean would have walked to Expedia rather than wait for the shuttle, he would already have been there. Of course, I did not say that to him as it would have only made him more upset.

Instead, I empathized with his situation and told him I would get him there in three minutes. Fortunately, we made it in just under two and a half minutes. Poor Sean. On top of his other woes, he had to pay an additional surge charge of two dollars and eighty-nine cents.

While I was on my way to pick up my next passenger, I got a text message from Lyft, reminding me about the *New Driver Welcome* that morning. The text message was actually preceded by several emails. The welcome event included dinner, a brief orientation and *Q&A*. I was never invited to any event from Uber. The shift from Uber to Lyft was looking easier by the minute.

Gloria

Pushing aside any feelings of Uber abandonment, I picked up Gloria and her daughter, Summer, at the Extended Stay America. Summer had a baby she was carrying in a baby seat. Mother, daughter and grandchild were on their way to Walmart for a shopping trip.

I asked if the two women were sisters. Whoops. Gloria was the mom and she loved my mix-up. Gloria then began talking to her daughter, occasionally stressing, I believe for my benefit, how she was a grandmother. I couldn't help but smile the entire trip.

Gloria then started to talk to Summer about the local schools. They had both been in town a week and were going to make Bellevue their home. When we passed one grade school, the daughter pointed, "Look, the schools are a lot smaller than the schools in North Carolina."

Gloria said, "That is true. But the classes here are smaller. So, it is better."

I enjoyed the two women so much, I decided I would interject, "That's right. The schools here are excellent. I have one daughter with a speech disability that has made remarkable progress. My two youngest daughters are both enrolled in dual immersion programs. They are now fluent in Chinese. The school district also has a couple of Spanish immersion schools. You will find the schools here are very progressive."

Gloria said to me, "That is good to know. We're moving here from North Carolina and are just getting ourselves oriented to the neighborhood."

The mother looked proud and the daughter looked confident. I dropped the happy trio off at Walmart. I wanted to tell Gloria but couldn't find the courage to say, I hope when my girls are older, that my relationship with them is as good as your relationship with Summer. Given how perceptive Gloria was, I think she might have known. No matter, I was off to pick up my next passenger.

Sashi

Sashi was on her way to HLC America on the Microsoft Campus. To this day, I am not sure what HLC America does. I went to their website and after reading their homepage, found myself even more in the dark.

I picked up Sashi at an apartment complex in Redmond. I could tell she was on a budget as she ate breakfast with one hand and held a container in her other hand. She had that starving college student vibe. When I dropped her off, I wasn't sure if I should give her money, maybe to help her with lunch.

Sahil

Quite possibly my last day with Uber, I was not yet ready to be done. So, I picked up Sahil at the Marriott in downtown Bellevue. Sahil had been interviewing for a job and was on his way to SeaTac to catch a flight to Los Angeles. I really enjoyed this young man. It was like reliving the excitement of my youth.

"Looking forward to going home?" I asked.

"A little," he said. "I've been doing job interviews in Bellevue, and I should know if I was successful by the time I get back."

"Are you working in California?" I enquired.

"No, I am going to school. I finished my undergraduate work in India, and I am now completing my graduate degree in computer science at the University of Southern California."

"That's impressive. So, when will you graduate? In December?"

"No, I will finish this spring. I just started looking for jobs and the interviews were stressful, so I am glad I started early."

I could hear the anticipation and dread of waiting for an offer in his voice. "Do you remember the excitement you felt when you were accepted at USC?" I asked. "Sahil, believe me, getting a job offer will be even more exciting. You will soon be a newly minted grad from the esteemed USC. You possess a warm and inviting persona and you obviously have a deep knowledge base. I have no doubt a corporation will be chomping on the bit to have you as a part of their team. So, believe me, that job offer will come. Your biggest problem will be knowing which job offer to accept. How will you know which job to take?"

I liked this young man, but at this point, I became truly surprised at Sahil's response. Sahil already developed his own personal philosophy. Sahil began by talking about the risks and rewards of today's job market. Sahil wanted to "live a life with minimum of regrets".

"That's very poetic," I said. "A life with minimum of regrets. I like that. Did you read that somewhere or did you come up with that yourself?"

"No," he said. "It is mine. Every action I take, I always reflect on whether it is something I might regret or something that will add meaning to my life."

I was overtaken by the sincerity and the kindness in his voice. I could hear an almost quiet pleading or prayer.

"I am very interested in living in this area," he continued. "I guess that is why I am so nervous."

"Have you looked at the cost of living here?"

"Yes, I know that the cost of living is high, but all of the jobs I am applying for are $100K+. They also include very generous relocation packages."

The young man seemed to have everything covered. What he probably didn't know was that when he got his dream job, tremendous challenges still lay ahead. But unlike so many young people I met, Sahil had a solid foundation for long term success. His philosophy of minimum regrets would see him through the most difficult of obstacles. I thought, I hope my daughters can find a Sahil in their life.

When Sahil stepped out of the car, I felt young again. Getting accepted into college, getting my first job, ahhhhhhh, the memories. Thank you, Sahil, for allowing me to both remember and feel those days again.

I was feeling a little sad, knowing I would not be driving for a couple of weeks. I had no idea what the Lyft driving experience would be like. But when I arrived home, I received the following email from Lyft.

> "Congrats on becoming an approved Lyft driver! Now that you've completed the Lyft application process, you

have a few last steps to comply with the City of Seattel, and King County's requirements.

Here's what you need to do:

1. Complete your Lyft Seattle Quiz. It's required, free and should only take a few minutes.

2. Pick up your for-hire permit. We're applying for one for you, so all you need to do is watch your inbox – we'll email you as soon as it's ready, normally in a few weeks.

3. Take your defensive driver course. We'll send you the link once you've been issued your for-hire permit.

4. Apply for the City of Seattle business license as soon as you start driving.

For more information, head to the Help Center. Thanks for staying compliant in Seattle. We'll see you on the road."

Lyft was not only welcoming me, they were keeping me up to date, providing valuable information and opportunities. Any sense of loyalty to Uber evaporated. I realized for the first time that what I enjoyed most about my driving experience was not Uber, but my passengers. Uber was just an app on a phone that allowed me to connect to my passengers.

Lyft was more than an app. Lyft, in my limited experience, reached out to their drivers, supporting them, encouraging them, treating them like human beings. Lyft was the experience I originally anticipated when I started driving for Uber. Somewhere, Uber decided drivers were a means to an end.

Lyft got it right. They seemed to understand that drivers are both the means and the end. I was now ready to go on vacation, and meet some fellow drivers.

Note: Elon Musk rolled out today Tesla's first fully electric truck. It looked awesome! And of course, enhanced autopilot came standard. Self-driving trucks! Things that make you go hmmmmmmm![22]

---

[22] https://www.wired.com/story/what-does-teslas-truck-mean-for-truckers/?mbid=email_onsiteshare

Part Two
LYFT OFF

CHAPTER NINE

DRIVER'S PERSPECTIVE

Uber said on Tuesday its British drivers will have to take a six-hour break after they have accepted and made trips with passengers totaling 10 hours as the taxi app responds to criticism over excessive working hours.

CNBC, January 16, 2018[23]

WORKING HARD FOR YOUR MONEY
November 18, 2017, Saturday

My immediate family was gathering in Orlando, Florida to celebrate Thanksgiving. The timing and place could not have been better, as my sixteen-year old stepdaughter would be playing in the national honor band. This year's location: Orlando, Florida. The vacation became the perfect opportunity for trips to Disney World, a family Thanksgiving celebration and my stepdaughter's national honor band concert. So, even though we rented a car, we had several opportunities to avail ourselves to Uber.

Our first Uber ride as passengers was from our home in Bellevue to the airport at Seatac. As there were four of us travelling with eight bags, I called for an UberXL, UberX's big brother. UberXL, an SUV or minivan, seats at least six and is more expensive than UberX. While my

---

[23] https://www.cnbc.com/2018/01/16/uk-uber-drivers-will-be-forced-to-take-breaks-between-long-shifts.html

family waited for our Uber, I received an email from Uber: "We're thankful for you Raymond."

I was confused. Was Uber starting to reach out to its drivers as human beings? Had the bad publicity finally caught up with Uber? Had I overreacted to Uber and my perceived neglect of Uber to their drivers?

I quickly caught my mistake. I was still operating in the "driver" mode and forgot that I was now the passenger. The email was not meant for Ray, the Uber driver, but Ray, the Uber passenger.

The email, in very large type, communicated three key facts concerning my relationship as an Uber passenger:

1. I had been using Uber a little over a year and a half;
2. I made fifteen trips over that time, and;
3. I had a high passenger rating.

It suddenly occurred to me that I was developing a love-hate relationship with Uber. I needed another opinion, as I was now completely biased as a driver. So, I asked Joyce to sit in the front seat and quietly interview the driver about their experience driving, while I sat in the back seat and took notes. Joyce agreed.

Dino

Joyce and I did a collective "Wow!" when Dino, driving a brand, new, black Lincoln MKC, pulled up. Dino was obviously proud of his car as he kept it in immaculate condition. As I stepped into the car, I noticed that the sleek interior was spotless.

Joyce got into the front seat while Julia, Emma, and I sat in the back. I complimented Dino on his car, to which Dino added, "And it has excellent gas mileage."

Joyce, true to her word, then asked Dino, "Do you live in Bellevue?"

"I live in Kent," Dino responded.

"Have you always lived in Kent?"

"In 1985, I moved from India to San Antonio, Texas. I liked San Antonio as it was affordable, but I did not like the weather. As there were few people from northern India in Texas, I made the decision to move my family to Washington State."

"Bellevue is quite the drive from Kent," Joyce reflected out loud, knowing that Kent was just over an hour away.

"Yes, but I spent the first sixteen years in Washington State living in Bellevue. The schools are great and all my children were able to take advantage of the Bellevue school district. But Bellevue became too expensive so we moved to Kent. We've been living in Kent the last four years as it's cheaper."

Joyce, listening to Dino's accent, asked him if he spoke any languages besides English. Dino spoke three other languages, Urdu, Punjab and Hindi. Urdu and Hindi have a lot of similarities, but Punjabi is a distinctly separate language.

"You probably did not know," Dino informed us, "that Hindi is the world's fourth most spoken language and Punjabi is the world's tenth most spoken language."

From the back seat, I acknowledged my ignorance of both Indian dialects as well as northern India. Dino was more than happy to educate us. "I lived in the state of Punjab, about 22 kilometers from the Pakistani border. In 1947, with the partition of the British Indian Empire, Punjab was divided in half. Half went to Pakistan and half went to India. Today, minorities are no longer safe."

Joyce asked, "What minorities?"

"In northern India," Dino responded, "minorities are Muslims, Christians and Sikhs. It is not safe as there is a lot of fighting between the minority groups. As I and my family are Sikhs, I made the decision to move to the United States."

"How often do you go back?" Joyce asked.

"I used to travel back and forth frequently. It has become too expensive. The last time I was in India was seven years ago."

Joyce, knowing more about northern Indian politics than I did, asked, "Do you feel more Punjabi or more Indian?"

Dino's answer was quick and direct. "Punjabi. But I have been in the United States since 1985 and I now feel more American. We are very lucky here as our problems are small compared to other countries. This county has good rules and good regulations."

At this point, I started to think that Joyce was straying from our original mission of discovering the Uber experience from the driver's perspective. I was wrong. The background of the driver is critical to our understanding, and Dino fit the profile of an Uber driver.

37% of drivers are white. 86% are male, 50% are married and 50% are over forty years old.[24] These were not the numbers I expected, but the demographic was certainly consistent with the drivers I met in my travels. So, thinking about the numbers, I sat back, and continued to take notes while Joyce continued.

At this point, Joyce's line of questions returned to our original purpose. "Why do you drive in Bellevue, rather than near your home in Kent or Seattle?" Joyce asked.

"I am familiar with Bellevue. Bellevue may have less business than Seattle, but it is safer. Seattle has more tickets, more accidents, more bad people."

"Do you like driving for Uber?" Joyce asked.

Dino hesitated, and then said, "Uber is okay, but it has gotten worse over the past several years. In 2013, 2014, and 2015, the money was good. But a lot of changes took place. Uber stopped listening to their drivers. Drivers began to make less and less money."

"Do a lot of drivers feel that way?" Joyce asked.

"Wait," Dino said as he removed his phone from its cradle. "I will show you a video that all the drivers are talking about."

It took a few moments for Dino to find the video on his phone. Turning the video on, Dino handed the phone to Joyce. The video was entitled, "Uber Slave".[25] The subtitle was "12 hours of driving for $140?" and it appeared to have resonated strongly with Dino.

The driver on the video, Corey, called Uber "slave labor", a form of "transportation sweat labor". Corey was pretty hot, predicting Uber

---

[24] https://www.entrepreneur.com/article/242096

[25] https://www.youtube.com/watch?v=4SfT-SO8Gjc

would drop him after he posted the video. Corey talked about Uber's increasing greed. He complained how no one tipped.

When the video ended, Dino looked seriously at Joyce and said, "Less than 1% of my customers have caused me trouble. But Uber, the company, does not respect their drivers. They no longer listen to their concerns."

Thinking about Dino's financial situation, I asked: "Have you ever thought of working for Lyft?"

Dino said, "I do not drive for Lyft. But I plan to apply next week as I no longer make enough money to make my house payment."

Joyce and I looked at each other in silent affirmation. I shared my hourly pay results with Joyce so we had a mutual appreciation for Dino's situation. Dino might have been making more as an XL driver, but it would still be hard to support a family.

As we entered the airport to catch a 6 am flight, I was amazed that at even at this early time in the morning, Joyce and I were completely mesmerized by Dino. When Dino dropped us off, he quickly got out of the car, rushed to get our bags, and brought them to the curb. Then, on parting, Dino turned to us and said, "God bless you. Have a safe trip. And happy Thanksgiving."

I thought, here is a better man than myself. I hope my girls are paying attention to him.

Because of Dino, I found myself quickly getting into the Thanksgiving spirit. I felt truly blessed, connected to a world so much larger and so much kinder than I typically acknowledged. When it came time to celebrate Thanksgiving with my family, I said my own prayer of thanks for Dino and his family.

When the option to tip Dino came up on my Uber app, I was presented with three choices, one dollar, five dollars, and ten dollars (somehow, I missed the option that said "Other"). I was going to give Dino a twenty-dollar tip, but being a little disoriented so early in the morning, I hit the ten-dollar option. It was my mistake for missing the option button, but I was in a hurry. It didn't stop me from thinking, damn that Uber.

THANKSGIVING EVE
November 23, 2017, Wednesday

Multiple news reports came out about Uber concealing a major data breach. Fifty-seven million customers and drivers were affected by the breach which Uber knew for well over a year. The hackers demanded one hundred thousand dollars from Uber to conceal the breach and delete the stolen data. Uber paid.

I started to imagine a typical day in Uber corporate leadership. The morning would be sales meetings, with an emphasis on profit margins. The afternoon would be marketing meetings where executives would update their investors on Uber's progress. Early evening would be a meeting with engineers for a progress report on their autonomous vehicles. The remaining time was left for any passenger or driver concerns. In other words, there just wasn't enough time in the day for the concerns of passengers and drivers. The duplicity of Uber was alarming.

It was fortunate on this Thanksgiving Eve that I had my second opportunity to take another ride as an Uber passenger. And it was both redeeming and rewarding that I would have Steven as my driver.

Steven

The Epcot Center at Disney World was closing, and a throng of people were making their way to the exit. Fully expecting to see a surge charge, I got on my Uber app and placed a call for the second Uber ride of our vacation. The Uber was six minutes away and to my amazement, no surge charge.

It was close to 10 pm when we were picked up by Steven in his Chrysler Town and Country. As we stepped into the luxury passenger van, I was delighted, once again, to find the car sparkly clean. Instead of a phone on a dock, Steven had an iPad docked to his dashboard. The iPad clearly showed the route to our destination and I noticed Steven easily went back and forth from the Uber app to Google maps. He was keeping his options open to the fastest route. From Steven's iPad, to the immaculate condition of the Steven's courteous manner, to the entire dashboard presentation, Steven was clearly a professional.

I looked at my watch and saw the time was 9:53 pm. I asked Steven how long he had been driving. "I started driving at 7:30 am," he said, as if he was talking about a drop in a bucket. "I took two hours off in the afternoon and have been driving ever since."

Steven was putting in a 12-hour day. "How many hours a week do you work?"

Steven paused, thought for a moment, then said, "I work six days a week, usually 12 hours a day, sometimes 14 hours a day. Because it is tourist season, the only time it is slow is between 12 pm and 3 pm, so sometimes I take a break during that time. I would say I probably put in 70 hours per week."

Right before I started driving for Uber, Joyce and I met David, the savvy bartender that used Uber to get paid to drive back and forth to his work place. I remembered hearing that most people driving for Uber worked part time. Now, for the second time in a row, I met a driver that was working ungodly hours just to make a living for himself and his family. I wanted to know more about Steven.

Steven emigrated from Brazil to the United States three years ago, and lived in Orlando since he first moved to the United States. Steven arrived with his wife and his step-daughter, who was now twenty-one years old. Steven helped raise his step-daughter since she was eight years old.

Joyce, a linguist herself, asked, "What languages do you speak?"

"I am fluent in three languages. Portuguese is my native language, English is my second language, and Spanish is my third language."

For the next few minutes, Joyce spoke to Steven in Spanish. I gave her a small nudge and she then, for my benefit, asked Steven in English, "Do you like driving?"

Steven loved driving as he felt it was the "best school" to improve both his Spanish and English.

Joyce asked Steven, "How long have you been working for Uber?"

"The first year, I worked at Lyft. Unlike Uber, Lyft did not require you to have a driver's license for one year before you could drive. Lyft later changed that rule and is now similar to Uber. I went to Uber after my first year because Uber has a car category that fits my class of car, a van, so I am able to make extra money."

"And how did you learn about Uber?" Joyce asked.

"I found out about Uber from a group of Brazilian drivers. The drivers meet a couple of times a month to discuss best practices."

I was immediately impressed by Steven's response as I remembered the mistakes I made during my first week of driving. I was not aware of any driver support group in the Bellevue area. Once again, Joyce and I were really enjoying our time with an Uber driver.

"I started by driving in Orlando," Steven continued. "I did pick-ups and drop-offs at the Orlando Airport. Sometimes, I would wait anywhere between an hour and an hour and a half for a fare as there were as many as 150 drivers at the airport. So, I started working nights at the bars in downtown Orlando. I had to deal with a lot of drunk people." Steven than pointed to a cam sitting on top of the middle of his front dash, and said, "I bought a dash cam because of the drunks."

"That's terrible," Joyce emphasized. "What's the worst thing that has ever happened to you on those drives?"

Steven thought for a moment. "There are so many bad experiences. But the worst one was when a husband punched his wife in my car. I immediately pulled over and called the police."

"That's incredible," Joyce said excitedly. "How did you know what to do?"

Steven, impressed by Joyce's interest, said, "When I was in Brazil, I worked as a police officer so I had pretty extensive training in these situations."

Sitting in the back, I couldn't keep silent. "Why did you leave Brazil and your career?"

Steven did not seem to mind our bombarding him with questions. "The job in Brazil," he said gravely, "was very dangerous. The people in Brazil do not have respect for the police like people do in the United States. When I was a police officer, we caught a member of a drug family. Because of the arrest, the entire family of one of the police officers was killed. It was then that I decided to leave Brazil."

That was a lot more information than the two of us bargained for. I was thinking witness protection? We spent the entire day in Disney World and our imaginations were running wild. We were going to be returning to our rental soon so Joyce decided to change course, "So, do you have plans beyond Uber?"

"Yes," Steven said. "I am hoping, to go back to college, so that I can return to public security, this time in the United States. But until I am able to do that, I have made some changes. I no longer drive in the city. I now Uber around the Disney parks because they are much safer."

While Steven was talking, I noticed earlier he closed out our fare eight minutes before our arrival. I wondered whether he was attempting to get another fare, if possible, maybe to get back to the Disney parks, but I did not ask as I was overtaken by his story on leaving Brazil. We were almost back when I saw that the fare cost a little over twenty-one dollars.

I looked at my app, this time looking for the custom tip option. I discovered the custom option besides the one dollar, five dollar, and ten dollar options. As it was the day before Thanksgiving and Steven's story was worth the trip alone, I left a twenty-dollar tip which Joyce wholeheartedly supported. Exiting the car, Joyce and I exchanged happy Thanksgiving wishes with Steven.

It was late, we were tired from a long day in the park, but Joyce and I were spellbound. Joyce and I found Steven to be a respectful and gentle man. It was a little like meeting an Uber super hero.

PREPARING FOR LYFT

November 28, 2017, Tuesday

Lyft provided me with three documents that I started to review. As I was on vacation, I decided to get a head start on the materials. The first was a glossy marketing piece on tax tips, the second was a piece on how to use the Lyft app (which I already reviewed), and the third, and maybe the most important was a to-do list.

Taxes and the Quickbooks Self-Employed App

The first document I reviewed was "Tax Tips for Lyft Drivers," a document created through a partnership between Lyft and Quickbooks. Quickbooks and Lyft developed an app called QuickBooks Self Employed. The app allows the driver to track miles, making it easy for the driver to record income and expenses for tax time. Quickbooks does the math so the driver knows exactly what they owe the IRS each quarter. No such information was provided by Uber.

I also learned that the standard IRS mileage rate for 2017 was 53.5 cents per mile. So, my educated guess of fifty cents per mile for expenses like gas, oil changes, repairs, and insurance was once again confirmed. Again, where was all this information before and after I started driving for Uber?

The To-Do List

Although I could start driving for Lyft, there were three items I needed to complete if I wanted to continue driving for Lyft. I needed to get a Seattle business license if I wanted to legally drive in Seattle; I needed to obtain a defensive driving certificate; and I needed to obtain a For-Hire Permit. My goal was to complete all three items before I returned from my vacation.

I was not sure if I needed a business license. I was operating out of Bellevue, so it was not clear to me whether I needed to do this so I texted to Lyft to find out. Lyft never responded.

The defensive driving certificate was a training module I could do online. I called State Farm and they said I could get a discount on my car insurance if I passed the course. That was an unforeseen perk.

The last item involved obtaining a For-Hire permit. Uber never mentioned anything about the For-Hire permit. Fortunately, Lyft would do the work in applying for the permit and would then contact me when I could pick it up. As the process takes three months, I had nothing to do but wait.

While I was reading through the materials, Lyft sent me an email offering me a paid, onsite training opportunity. Shocking! I was not provided anything close to training, much less paid training by Uber.

To be fair, Uber did offer a drivers' dinner that night, which I could not attend from Orlando. But the dinner was a first for Uber, and appeared to be a reaction to all of the company's bad publicity. I was curious as to what Uber would disclose at the dinner. What would Uber say about the hack Uber covered up for a year? Dinner, I thought, is the least Uber could do.

Dino, our Uber driver, told us he enjoyed his passengers, but he really disliked Uber. This was a statement I would continue to hear over and over from other drivers. Even with Uber's bad press, I am not sure if passengers can truly appreciate the moral bankruptcy taking place at Uber. Given Uber's size and branding, it was more likely that Uber's deception and cover-up, like all of the other controversies surrounding Uber, would be quickly forgotten. Would I forget and drive for Uber again? I hoped not.

Asad

November 30, 2016, Thursday

Vacation came to an end and I was getting excited to once again get behind the wheel, this time, as a Lyft driver. Our plane landed in Seattle, so we decided to take Lyft to get the family back home. Frankly, I had my fill of Uber, so while I was in Orlando, I downloaded the Lyft passenger app. It would be my first time using Lyft as a passenger.

Once again, we were four people, but now with ten bags (thank you, Disney). I requested a Lyft Plus, "a car that seats 6 or more passengers."[26] We did not have to wait long.

Asad, who lives in SeaTac, picked us up in his new Toyota Highlander. A mid-size crossover, the black, sporty Highlander was spacious. I heard driving cars in the UberXL and Lyft Plus category can be as high as ten dollars more per hour for drivers. That would make

---

[26] https://www.ridesharingdriver.com/whats-the-difference-between-lyft-lyftplus-and-line/

the annual salary $52,000 a year for the driver with little to no benefits. It was certainly a jump from the $31,000 a year the UberX driver was making.

Asad's car was the nicest car to date. The drive home was a couple dollars less than our Uber trip to the airport, even though the Lyft trip was almost seven minutes longer due to traffic. I heard Lyft was cheaper than Uber, but here was verification right out of the gate.

Asad just started a month ago and was driving, like many of the drivers, for both Uber and Lyft. "Which one do you like more?" Joyce asked.

"Lyft," he responded. "They have good bonuses."

Bonuses, I thought, would be helpful, given Uber's low pay. Bonuses might even supplement drivers' losses when making a return trip with an empty car. Asad's comment reinforced to me why an increasing number of drivers were shifting from Uber to Lyft. Drivers needed to keep the Lyft app and the Uber app on to decrease wait times and avoid riding home empty handed. Given the inflated earnings presented by both Uber and Lyft, drivers needed to be pretty savvy.

Joyce asked Asad, "Where are you from?"

"I grew up in Somalia, but have been living in Washington state for the past 22 years."

"So, you have family here?"

"Yes," Asad said proudly. "I am married and have 8 children, 5 boys and 3 girls. The oldest is 20 and the youngest is just 4 years old."

"That's a big family to support," Joyce marveled.

"I put in long hours. I also support my mother in Somalia. I send her five hundred dollars every month. But right now, with the exception of one son, my family is living in Kenya where they are operating a business."

"That must be hard," Joyce said with concern in her voice.

"No, it is okay," Asad said. "There is no electronic stuff in Kenya which is better for the children."

Joyce shared with Asad that we had four daughters, and I added: "I wish I had eight," which seemed to establish an immediate bond between Asad and me.

"It is better to have a lot of children," he said. "They are like insurance. Children take care of parents. It is part of my religion (Islam). To have an abortion is murder. You agree with me, Raymond."

Sitting in the back seat of the car, I was distracted by the sound of traffic and rain so I could understand only about half the conversation. I did not catch the abortion statement, but responded back empathetically, "Yes."

Asad sat up in his seat, a big smile on his lips, and proclaimed, "Yes!"

I thought I might have dodged a bullet and Joyce confirmed to me later I indeed had. Joyce immediately took back control of the conversation. "What did you do on Thanksgiving?"

"I worked Thanksgiving. The holiday was busy. Except it took 30 minutes just to get in to the airport."

"What did you do before you drove for Lyft?" Joyce asked.

"I worked for the Port of Seattle," he said. "My father died last year and I returned to Somalia for six months. Most jobs are not flexible enough to take that much time away, so I started working for Lyft and Uber."

"How many hours are you working now?" I asked.

"I work 9 hours a day with a 1 hour break, "Asad explained. "I earn about three hundred dollars and then I go home."

"Is driving safe?" Joyce asked.

"For the most part, yes. I try to stay away from Seattle."

"We've heard from other drivers that driving in the Seattle area can be more dangerous, do you find that to be the case?"

"There are a lot of drunk people in Seattle. And on Saturday nights, it can be really bad."

"That makes sense," Joyce said as Asad pulled up to our building.

Asad pulled over, jumped out of the car, went to the back, and quickly brought our bags to the curb. He waved me aside in my feeble attempt to help. I felt guilty as one bag was sixty-eight pounds and another bag was forty-five pounds. As this was my first time using the Lyft app, I was not going to make the same mistake I made previously when I gave Dino a ten-dollar tip due to my unfamiliarity with the app.

I pulled out my wallet, grabbed a twenty-dollar bill, and wished Asad a happy holiday. He returned the greeting, got back into his car, and took off for his next fare.

Lyft, here I come!

CHAPTER TEN

CONTROL, WE HAVE A PROBLEM

CHANGING SIDES
December 1, 2017, Friday

Trips	Time on Road	Miles	Earnings	Vehicle Cost	Real Earnings	Hourly Wage
2	59	21	$23.49	-$10.50	$12.99	$13.21

After almost two weeks in Florida, my family returned late Thursday evening. Everyone was exhausted. I would take the weekend to recuperate and start driving for Lyft the following Monday. Or at least that was the plan.

Friday morning came and I couldn't wait to get back on the road. As soon as I dropped the girls off at the bus stop, my curiosity got the best of me, and I turned on the Lyft app.

Catherine

Just like Uber of old, I was immediately greeted with a passenger request. Great start. The location was an apartment just off Main Street in downtown Bellevue.

The ride did not start as smoothly as I hoped. Once again, like my initial experience with the Uber app, I initially fumbled with the Lyft app. Lyft does not have its navigation system embedded in its app like Uber. Instead, Lyft uses the Google map app. I found it a little tough having to flip back and forth between the Lyft app and Google maps. I was getting frustrated and I did not want to keep Catherine, sitting quietly in the back of the car, waiting. So instead, I just made a full confession. "Catherine, this is my first day with Lyft and I am having a difficult time with the app. Can you tell me your destination?"

Catherine smiled at my candor and said, "Oh, yes, no problem. I am going to work in Seattle. I can direct you there."

"Thank you! Do you always use Lyft to go to work?"

"Oh, no. About six months ago, my car was broken into. I had to park my car on the street as parking was too expensive in Bellevue. After the break-in, I decided to sell the car and use public transportation. Today, I'm taking Lyft because I missed my bus."

Catherine, a hairstylist, appeared to be enjoying life without a car. But after a few minutes, I could tell she was one of those people that knew how to appreciate any experience. She also had a long day ahead of her.

Catherine was attending the grand opening of the hair salon where she worked. She was excited about the party that was to take place that evening, saying, "The nice thing about Seattle is the dedication people have to shopping and buying local. For the grand opening, they are using all local products, like straight bourbon whiskey from Woodinville and gin from Bothell."

Catherine was wonderful. We talked the entire way, about her boyfriend, her job as a hairstylist, and the grand opening that evening. Her stories, both as a hairstylist and a former bartender, were reminiscent of the stories told by Mario, my barber.

"It is amazing what people will tell me," she said. "I still do not understand how I can meet a person once and they open up about the most personal details of their life. Just recently, I had one person, a mother, confide in me that she did not love her adopted child. I had no idea what to do with that piece of information."

I could tell Catherine liked people. She was easy to talk with, helpful in my early predicament with the app, and both reassuring and affirming – skills well cultivated through her work as a hairstylist. Catherine shared with me, "I'd like to buy a house here," and then grew thoughtfully silent for a moment. "But I know it is too expensive."

Given Catherine's positive disposition, I said, "I believe, especially for a person like yourself, it is possible. You have a strong will and such a positive energy. You are a dream-maker."

Catherine thanked me and gave me the sweetest smile. She reminded me how parents want the best for their children. Parents talk about their kids growing up to be doctors, lawyers, etc. As Catherine stepped out of the car, I thought, I would like my girls to grow up to be like Catherine.

Wrap Up

I took one more fare as I was in Seattle. It was a short drive and the passenger was quiet the entire journey. But overall, I had a great day, both personally and financially. On my first ride, my earnings were eighteen dollars and seventy cents including a three-dollar tip (thank you, Catherine!). On my second and last ride, my earnings were four dollars and sixty-nine cents including a dollar tip. Lyft was certainly different as both passengers tipped me.

As Asad told me, Lyft also offers a lot of incentives in the way of bonuses. Right off the bat, Lyft offered a number of ways I could receive a cash bonus. The first potential bonus had to do with acceptance rates. The second bonus had to do with peak rides, similar to Uber's surge pricing. The third bonus had to do with completing 70 rides.

All the bonuses were clearly marked on the app, providing my own personal progress report. Once I completed sixty-eight more rides (I wasn't quite sure I would be driving that long), I would receive a four hundred and twenty-five-dollar bonus. After two hundred drives, a five-hundred-dollar sign-on bonus kicked in. Lyft knew how to cater to its drivers.

Defensive Driving Course

When I returned home, I started the online Defensive Driving Course required by both Lyft and Uber. There was no reimbursement for the time it took to go through the training, and the training was between six and eight hours. If you pass the test, neither Lyft nor Uber offered any kind of bonus. With the exception of a possible reduction on one's car insurance, the course was another out of pocket expense for the driver.

I did not think I would like the course. I had been driving for almost forty years. What could it teach me? Once again, I was, fortunately in this case, wrong. I enjoyed the Defensive Driving Course. Did you know:
- The Number of mature drivers (55+) is increasing by 19% every ten years.
- There is almost a 10% chance of getting into car accident every year.
- Over half of fatal accidents occur with individuals 70 or older.
- Every day in the US, 13 young people die in an alcohol-related collision.
- 54% of people killed in accidents are unrestrained.
- 90% of child safety seats are installed incorrectly.
- Even in 60-degree temperature, temp inside a car can become life threatening in minutes.

The course was challenging and I could tell it would take about eight hours to complete. I would not hurry the course. I would go slowly and complete it over the next week. I could tell the course was helping me to appreciate my own role in creating a safe and friendly place on the road. Smiling to myself, I thought, how do I get my daughters to take the course?

BAD START
December 4, 2017, Monday

Trips	Time on Road	Miles	Earnings	Vehicle Cost	Real Earnings	Hourly Wage
1	1 hr 4 min	4	$3.44	-$2.00	$1.44	$1.35

I was on the clock for one hour and received only one ride. The ride only lasted six minutes, and once again, more technical difficulties. I talked to a couple of drivers that stopped driving for Lyft because of the app alone. They, like myself, did not like switching back and forth between the Lyft app and the navigation app.

Alex

When I picked up Alex, I found myself once again fumbling with the app. Every time I touched the navigation button, I was taken to Google maps. Google maps would then tell me to enter the destination again which I tried to do, but to no avail. I returned to the Lyft app. I was again taken to Google maps, but the navigation did not start immediately and I still had Alex waiting in the car.

Nothing else I could do, the poor guy had to give me directions. As Alex was occupied on his phone, this did not work out well. I drove past his destination without him even realizing it.

I told Alex I would do a U-turn, but he told me not to worry. He would walk the block. Poor customer service on my part. And to be expected... No tip.

I pulled over and went back to the Lyft tutorial. After reviewing the tutorial a second time, it looked like there might be a glitch in my app, so I deleted the app and then downloaded the app once again. My app was now working properly.

I waited and waited, but no other calls came in for a ride. I basically sat on my hands for just over an hour to earn what amounted to one dollar and thirty-five cents an hour. I thought about turning the Uber app on in order to drum up more business, but, still sickened by the constant plague of problems and deception that followed Uber, I took the moral high ground and refrained. As I did not depend on this work for my mortgage, my car payment, or even my coffee at Starbucks, I had the luxury of making a decision based on my social justice convictions. I was in the minority. But if this continued, would I be able to hold out?

It was becoming increasingly obvious to me that to be a successful driver, one needed both Uber and Lyft. Lyft made some significant progress in market share, but drivers still depended on Uber's income as passengers continued to rely on Uber's convenience and its historic brand dominance. I might very well have to turn on both apps, at least for this rideshare experience. I was becoming more and more appreciative of these underpaid travel warriors.

THE DARK SIDE
December 5, 2017, Tuesday

Trips	Time on Road	Miles	Earnings	Vehicle Cost	Real Earnings	Hourly Wage
9	4 hr 1 min	67	$65.56	-$33.50	$32.06	$7.98

I got on the road early at 6:20 am, the earliest I ever started. I made the decision to drive completely through the surge times in a quest to earn three hundred dollars in a day. Today was the day.

The day did not go as planned. I was defeated almost immediately out the gate. It was definitely a defeat of my own making. After two Lyft trips, I stopped getting Lyft fares, so I, the hypocrite, turned on the Uber app. Maybe the gods were taking their revenge after all I said about Uber. For the rest of the day, I did not see another fare request from Lyft. My final five trips were Uber and in what appeared to be cruel fate, two of those rides were the dreaded UberPool. But I am getting ahead of myself.

Sean

My first passenger, Sean, was a stroke of good luck as he was staying at the AC Hotel, right across the street from where I live. As soon as Sean got into the car, he was on his computer, typing away. He was incredibly busy for 6:30 am which I found commendable. His destination was the Andaluca Restaurant, a fine Mediterranean eatery in Seattle. I assumed a business meeting.

Approaching Seattle, I noticed that the city was all decked out for the holidays. Even Sean glanced up from his computer to take in the stunning display of sparkling lights crowned by a large Christmas tree sitting atop the Seattle Space Needle. At one stoplight, I even pulled my phone from its dock to take a picture of one exceedingly festive scene, but almost immediately put my phone back in the dock. This would not be safe, I thought, once again realizing I indeed learned something from my defensive driving course.

Maria

After dropping Sean off, I made a quick U-turn and headed to my next passenger, Maria. I pulled up behind a pick-up truck. Maria was nowhere to be found. My phone rang and it was Maria.

"Where are you?" she said.

"I'm out front."

"Park behind the pick-up truck in front of my apartment building."

"I am already behind the pick-up truck."

Maria responded, "No, you are not."

It was only then I realized I was actually behind a car that was behind the pick-up truck. I apologized and said, "There is a car behind the pick-up truck. I am parked behind that car."

Maria hung up, walked out of her building, spotted my car, walked over, and pointed at the car between myself and the pick-up truck and said, "I told you."

I apologized once again. Maria then proceeded to give me turn by turn directions which I followed. She repeated everything my navigation system was stating aloud. I was now receiving directions in stereo. When we arrived, Maria got out of the car and, without looking back, descended into her coffee shop.

I have to admit, I was thoroughly entertained by her somewhat anal behavior. I sensed she enjoyed bossing me around. It was like driving a dominatrix.

I drove on for a block or two and pulled into a parking spot.

I waited for another Lyft passenger to no avail. I made the blasphemous decision to turn on the Uber app.

Right away, I was connected to a passenger and thus my descent back into Uber Hell. If it was Star Wars, I chose the dark side. I turned off the Lyft app and made my way to my Uber passenger.

Virginia

When I arrived in front of the house, Virginia, a young woman full of energy, came running, or should I say dancing down the driveway. She was absolutely wonderful, a vision of elegant joy at 7:30 in the morning.

Virginia just moved into the house which she shared with two men, who happened to be brothers. She was running because she was late to work. "That is a great place," I commented.

"Oh, I only rent a room," she said sweetly. "I have two roommates, brothers from Texas. They are also renting."

"How is that working out?" I asked.

"Good. Their parents, from east Texas, just visited. You know, east Texas is very red."

"I think a better word might be rural," to which she nodded.

"I pretty much had to keep my mouth shut for the entire visit," she lamented.

"Okay," I said, "you were right, red is probably the better word."

Virginia laughed. She started to hum along with the car stereo when she said, "Wow, you are playing holiday music. That is the first time this year I've heard holiday music."

"I find it very soothing," I said. "It takes the edge off the stress of driving in rush hour traffic. Plus, it has been a very rough year in this country."

She wholeheartedly agreed. What a pleasure to see such youth, hope, and exuberance so early. It felt like unwrapping a gift on Christmas morning. I was paying too much attention to Virginia when I blindly accepted another ride.

Jimmy

It was at this moment when all of my plans for a three-hundred-dollar day went by the wayside. I unknowingly accepted an UberPool. The ride took twenty-three minutes, taking me outside of Seattle, the hotspot of surge pricing, with only one passenger. No pool.

A growing number of cost conscious passengers will take Uber pool. Not only is it less expensive for the passenger, but they can get lucky when there are no other pool passengers. In these situations, they get a direct trip to their destination at a fraction of the price. An already squeezed driver ends up being paid far less then the normal fare.

I did learn you could take Martin Luther King Drive all the way from Seattle to Renton. It was one of those things I really didn't need to know. I was headed out of Seattle to Renton and Martin Luther King had some pretty bad neighborhoods.

Jimmy, my uberpool passenger, stepped into my car, wearing baggy sweats, smelling of alcohol and breathing heavy. He was on his way to a grade school. I had no idea why Jimmy was going to a grade school and Jimmy did not say one word the entire trip. When we arrived at the grade school, Jimmy got out of the car and, without so much as a good-bye, started walking toward the entrance of the school.

What to do next? There would now be heavy traffic and I would most likely miss a good chunk of the surge hours. I decided to return to Seattle. Then it happened. I was tagged for another ride. I would not have to go back empty-handed. In my excitement, once again without really looking, I accepted the ride.

Rebekah

Oh my God! I did it again. I picked up another UberPool rider, and again, there would be no other riders. How could I be so stupid! For the second time in a row, I found myself picking up a pool rider with no pool. A great savings to the rider but once again, a cost to the driver. I vowed to myself, never again, would I do another pool ride.

I was steamed but quickly changed my attitude when I greeted Rebekah. Rebekah, a high school student, was on her way to school. It seems like everyone is doing rideshare now, I thought. I enjoyed the experience of taking a high school student to school, as it reminded me how much I missed my stepdaughter Sophia, who was finishing her senior year in North Dakota, and my stepdaughter Kiana, who was on her study abroad program in China.

Rebekah seemed to thoroughly enjoy our short trip. I once again marveled that even high school students were using rideshare to get to school. Maybe, I thought, my day had turned around.

Juliana

After a long drive back to Seattle, I was a little frustrated as I had been doing a lot of "dead" driving during the few peak/surge hours. The clock was ticking and I was driving without a passenger. I then picked up Juliana, not an UberPool, (you should be able to hear my sigh of relief at this point). Finally, I was getting back on track.

Juliana, a young woman on her way to work, was both delightful and good humored. It was a short trip, although we did face a couple of obstacles. We ran into not one, but two closed streets. We tackled the closed streets together. Juliana was amazing, strategizing with me on various options to get her to work. After I dropped Juliana off, and being close to I-90, I decided to return to Bellevue.

As I got off I-90 and entered Bellevue Way, I got another UberPool request. Victory! I declined the UberPool request. That felt good. No, it felt great!

Both the Uber app and Lyft app were on and I was praying to get another Lyft trip. No one was answering my prayers. Finally, the Uber god answered.

James

I proceeded to pick up James in what might be the swankiest neighborhood in Bellevue. The house was hard to find as it sat in a remote area on a cliff. The house had breathtaking views of both Lake

Washington and Seattle. It was an enjoyable experience just being lost in the neighborhood.

When I arrived, James, a young man, stepped into the car. Like so many of my passengers, he was glued to his phone. I dropped James off at the Bellevue Pro Club, and before I could turn on the Lyft app, I received another Uber request from a passenger staying at the Westin in downtown Bellevue. Was my fate tied to Uber?

Didam

I drove to the Westin and waited for Didam. I looked around and the only person waiting was an attractive woman in her early thirties, talking on her phone. No Didam.

I thought, I will wait another minute, and then call him. At that very moment, the young woman, still talking on her phone, tapped on the passenger's side window. Aha! I mused. It must be Didam. I assumed incorrectly that Didam was a man's name.

Didam was professionally, yet fashionably dressed. When she entered my car, a strong fragrance engulfed me. Didam was beaming.

While Didam seat-belted herself into the back seat of the car, I took the time to notice that she was no longer talking on her phone, but listening to music, wearing headphones and tapping her fingers on her knee. I looked closer. She appeared nervous. I decided to check out her destination and was immediately delighted to see that I was taking another young person to the Microsoft recruiting building.

It was fun watching the self-confident young woman stride into the building. I could do this trip all day long. I looked at the clock and saw I already put in four hours. Although I had only made sixty-five dollars, I knew I could extrapolate from the numbers what I would make if I worked a full eight hours. I called it a day and returned home.

Driver Earnings

I was busy for just over four hours. Yet, even if I added another forty dollars in revenue to make up for the two UberPool rides, it would still be hard to earn even two hundred dollars in an eight-hour day. And then I would still have to deduct expenses. One would have to be a Jedi, trained in the art of surge driving, to get even close to three hundred dollars per day. Worse, after four hours, I was feeling a little sore.

What happened? Driving had been a breath of fresh air. I got to meet new people. Driving gave me a welcome opportunity to get out of the house, and I was able to make a few dollars. Working almost four hours, trying to hustle up three hundred dollars, I turned adventure into misadventure.

I cannot imagine what it would be like to drive for eight to ten hours per day, five to six days per week. What must it really be like for the drivers I met, attempting to make a full-time living out of driving? I felt horrible. I met so many outstanding drivers, trying to pay their bills and feed their families, working long hours, in an uncomfortable and a stressful environment.

As a part-time job, the pay and the hours are flexible. A full-time job? I did not think so.

Worse, I could not drive for Lyft alone. Sure, Lyft was making great strides in the marketplace. Google announced a billion-dollar investment in Lyft. Yet, Uber branding was still the dominant force.

I felt bad for my passengers. I knew how difficult it was for them to change their purchasing patterns. I was frustrated. I had become part of the problem. I was saddened by my dependence and other drivers' dependence on Uber.

I was not about to end the day without a success. I returned home and completed the online defensive driving course. When I passed the test, I called State Farm and received the discount on my car insurance as promised. All good things come to those that wait.

Lyft had one last surprise for me. Late that night, I received an email from Lyft inviting me and three others of my choosing to a Driver Holiday Celebration. A little bit of redemption on such a low day. The Lyft celebration included a holiday light show, photos with Santa, hot cocoa and more at Wild Waves Theme and Water Park. Once again, Lyft recognized its employees. Keep gaining that market share from Uber, Lyft!

CHAPTER ELEVEN

DEAL WITH THE DEVIL

THE RIDESHARE GOD
December 6, 2017, Wednesday

Trips	Time on Road	Miles	Earnings	Vehicle Cost	Real Earnings	Hourly Wage
3	63	25	$27.31	-$12.50	$14.81	$14.10

UBER			
Rides	Passenger Payment	UBER Earnings	Ray's Revenue
1	$6.42	$2.51	$3.46

LYFT			
Rides	Passenger Payment	LYFT Earnings	Ray's Revenue
1	$13.65 + $3.00 tip = $16.65	-$3.41	$13.24
2	$4.14	-$1.04	$3.10

I turned on the Lyft app and prayed to the rideshare god that I would not have to turn on the Uber app. Someone was listening. I ended the day with two rides from Lyft and one ride from Uber.

As I stepped over to the "dark side", I thought it would be interesting to compare the cost between the two businesses, so I broke the fares down as to what the passengers paid, what the rideshare companies earned and what I earned.

Marc

Initially, the rideshare god heard my plea and I picked up Marc, who lived off Bellevue's Main Street, a stone's throw away from the downtown park. Marc was headed off to work at Microsoft. I was in the mood for talking, but as soon as Marc entered the car, he was reading, then typing on his phone. I decided not to interrupt him.

Right before we got on to the highway, my wife, who had her annual physical at 7 am, called to let me know that her health was fine. I told her the news was great, that I had a passenger in the car, and that I would call her later. When I got off the phone, I immediately apologized to Marc, who responded, "No problem."

I thought Marc might think I was apologizing about taking a call from my wife who was reporting back on the results from a visit to her doctor. That would be pretty harsh on my part. I was actually apologizing for the fact that I would always take that call. Was I becoming an activist driver?

As we turned off the highway, I glanced back and saw that Marc was taking a break from his phone. I decided to ask him a question. "Can I ask you why you chose Lyft?"

Marc did not miss a beat, "The rides are faster, the drivers are nicer, and you guys are a bit more economical. Today, I was running late to work. So, I called Lyft as it is a personal trip."

"Do you use Lyft exclusively?"

"I have to use Uber with business because they sync with our expense reports. With Uber, I use my corporate card and the expenses show up on my report app with everything filled in so I don't have to enter anything manually. It is a weird convenience thing. And the company would rather us take Uber than a taxi for liability reasons."

I was fascinated, "Can I ask what you do?"

"I work at the Bravern for Microsoft," he replied. "I am a program manager in Microsoft's product division. I work on a startup team, so we work some pretty long hours."

"Sounds like an intensive job," I said

"On a scale of intensive jobs, it's not too bad. It is nothing like driving people all day. There is no risk to my life or limb. You know," Marc disclosed, "I drove for Uber for one day."

"You're kidding," I said skeptically.

"Yes, I was an Uber driver for one night. I just bought a brand-new car and thought about making some extra money. The car still had that new car smell. I drove on a Friday night and there were way too many drunk people. I drove my car like five times. I was terrified someone was going to throw up in it. Someone even scolded me for not having bags in the car to throw up into. I was like, whoa, excuse you."

"You are right," I agreed. "I have the luxury of not working evenings. I forget sometimes about the risks. Not to mention there are some really aggressive drivers on the road."

Marc nodded, "My dad, when he came to the United States, worked in a factory. He had all kinds of menial jobs. Driving is just the new version of that, you know, forty years ago. Just like companies back then, I know that Uber doesn't invest in their drivers. A lot of the companies are just biding times until they get automated cars. The drivers are treated like indentured servants."

I was impressed. Who was this guy putting forth so clearly the reality of today's driver? I asked one question and out popped verification of my driving experiences. Marc could have been reading my mind.

We arrived on Campus and I wished I started talking with Marc earlier. On exiting the car, Marc asked me my name. After I told him, he shook my hand and thanked me for the ride. Marc had a fourteen-dollar fare and tipped me three dollars. Class act.

David

I drove back to Bellevue from Redmond and as the Lyft god had not offered up any passengers, I turned on Uber. Boom! Uber responded and I picked up David at the Westin. I took David to the Microsoft Campus in complete silence as he was busy working on his phone. Okay, one more ride. I turned on both apps, rolled the dice and came up Lyft.

Elena

I was still riding high from my drive with Marc when I picked up Elena, whom happened to be at the same high rise where Joyce worked. I enjoyed the coincidence. Elena was one of those power professionals. She was on the phone, conducting an interview, and getting a ride at the same time.

Elena stepped into my car, still talking on her phone. I heard her say something like "My Uber arrived. I will do your interview offline."

Part of me enjoyed how passengers took ownership of both their rides and their drivers. But in this case, Elena was taking a Lyft, not an Uber as she indicated on the phone. Again, the power of the Uber brand. I could not escape it.

Elena's destination was her apartment just outside of downtown Bellevue. The ride took under three minutes. Maybe we were soul mates, but we covered a lot of ground. Elena intrigued me.

Elena worked several jobs, including being a writer for the Huffington Post. If I was a plumber, I would not be surprised to find out that Elena negotiated contracts for Restoration Hardware. Elena had her hands in everything.

Somehow, we got to talking about our holiday plans. While I was going to spend three weeks with my in-laws in New York, Elena was going to spend three weeks with her family in London. Elena was going on my dream vacation.

I told Elena I was hoping to travel to London and Marrakesh while in New York, but it was just too expensive. Elena told me she was going to fly from London to Morocco and spend one week of her holiday in Marrakesh. I was green with envy.

She continued, "I am also going to spend some time in Edinburgh."

"You're kidding me," I exclaimed. "That was the other location I priced out. I thought the fares would be lower since how many people are going to travel to the Highlands in the winter? It appears Edinburgh is a popular place over the holidays. Really, Elena, I have some strong vacation envy going on."

Elena smiled mischievously, "Since I will already be with family in London, it is a short train ride to Edinburgh," as if trying to let me know that her trip was doable as she was already in London. But really, London, Edinburgh and Marrakesh for the holidays? It was like someone just informed me that they opened my Christmas presents.

By the time I pulled into her apartment complex, I was seriously jealous of Elena. It was the first time I was jealous of any passenger. Elena was young, talented, and taking my dream vacation.

Elena stirred up a lot of emotion in me. I was amazed at how many feelings I was experiencing as a driver. I was angry, excited and hopeful at the same time. When I was driving on my own time, not concerned about how many hours I put in or how much money I made, driving was fun. It was addictive.

As I had a ton of content from my trips, I made the decision to end the day. It felt good. I bonded with Marc, and I was totally infatuated by Elena's life, all in sixty-one minutes. I earned twenty-seven dollars and thirty-once cents, okay, or fourteen dollars and ten cents an hour. But what a great way to begin the day. I wondered if my driving experience was what Marc hoped to achieve during his one Friday night Uber driver experience?[27]

ST. NICK
December 7, 2017, Thursday

Trips	Time on Road	Miles	Earnings	Vehicle Cost	Real Earnings	Hourly Wage
3	1 hr 18m	27	$30.36	-$13.50	$11.86	$12.97

LYFT			
Rides	Passenger Payment	LYFT Earnings	Ray's Revenue
1	$5.56+$2.00 tip = $7.56	-$1.39	$6.17
2	$14.45+$3.00 tip = $17.45	-$3.61	$13.84

---

[27] <u>Note</u>: Just finished an article that Lyft has launched its first self-driving service, in Boston. The service is limited to Boston's Seaport, and the cars are not completely driverless as Lyft tests out this new technology. But the end of taxi drivers is near.

Girls safely on the school bus, I decided I would only use the Lyft app. On a bright and sunny Seattle day, it was a good day for Lyft. I went three for three, and there was little to no wait time between the trips.

Alexis

I picked up Alexis at an apartment complex in downtown Bellevue. Alexis had not arrived, so I got out, opened the back door and waited for her. Lyft provides an actual wait time on the app, sometimes two minutes, sometimes five minutes. The two-minute wait time on the app was about to expire when I read something like, "When the wait time expires, drive off as there are other passengers waiting."

Wow, I thought. That seems a little harsh. They could at least suggest making a phone call to the passenger first. The wait time expired and I thought maybe I should wait another couple of minutes when I got a call from Alexis, she would be right down.

I could tell Alexis was delighted to have the door opened for her. I closed the door, walked around the car, got in and scrolled down to Alexis' destination, the hospital. Bummer. I asked her if she would like me to change the temperature in the car, usually a good conversation starter. Alexis thanked me and told me the temperature was fine. She then sat back, looking quietly out the window.

Alexis appeared to be in good spirits. But I always felt a little concerned when I drove people to the hospital. I wanted to know Alexis' story. But my passengers are like Christmas gifts, some come open, some stay wrapped. I was delighted when I got home and saw that Alexis left me a two-dollar tip. But I would have loved to have heard her story.

Talia

My next passenger was Talia who I picked up at the W in downtown Bellevue. It always surprised me when I pick up several people as the app only identifies one name. Two men slipped into the back of the car and Talia stepped into the passenger's seat next to me, while the valet from the W placed two suitcases and a large box in the trunk of my car. One man was from Berlin and the other man was from San Francisco. All professionally dressed, the two men in back conversed, completely ignoring Talia.

It seemed to me that the three passengers were together. They took the same ride, were staying at the same hotel, were all professionally dressed, and were going to the same Microsoft building. Why the division between the two men in the back and Talia in the front? At the very least, it seemed that just out of professional courtesy, Talia would be involved in the conversation, if only for social purposes. I proceeded to drive, curious to see whether the two men would involve Talia in their conversation.

Nope, it wasn't going to happen. As we neared the Microsoft Campus, Talia had another idea on how to get to their building. When I showed Talia the directions provided by the app, she said, "Oh, that is much better. I will trust you."

I told Talia, "Thank you for your trust. But I want you to know that I am trusting the app. The data provided to Google maps will often reroute me around heavy traffic." And with that, I had no idea how, we got into a conversation about trust.

I was a little amazed that we were having a conversation about trust as her colleagues in the back seat continued to ignore us. Talia started to talk to me about her mother who was living in Florida. Talia said, "My mother does not trust the way I drive. She doesn't trust me."

I responded, "Well, I imagine you will always be your mom's baby. But I bet that when your mother is with her friends, she probably tells them about how much trust and faith she has in you."

Talia laughed, agreeing wholeheartedly. I felt bad for this professionally dressed young lady, with mixed feelings of her self-worth, sharing intimate facts about her life with a Lyft driver. I wanted to praise Talia for her presence, being a successful woman in what is still very much a man's world. But her two colleagues were in the back, and like always, my job, at least now, was to park.

I took their two suitcases and heavy box out of the trunk. I wished them a good day and headed back to Bellevue.

Nicholas

When I saw the name, Nicholas. I immediately thought, good old St. Nick. I looked forward to picking up Nicholas just because of his name. Was it fair to Nicholas? Probably not. But come on, legendary gift giver, the original super hero, I couldn't help myself.

Nicholas lived in an apartment close to the high rise where I lived. Nicholas was sullen, almost brooding. Like so many of my passengers, he was a Microsoft employee on his way to work. I wanted to tell Nicholas the story of St. Nick. Again, Lyft driver.

So instead, un-jolly, not so St. Nick, stared distractedly into his phone while I drove. Seemed like I hit a critical mass in terms of my morning drives. The vast majority of my passengers were Microsoft employees, or Microsoft consultants, glued to their phones. It was with some relief when I dropped off St. Nick.

As I reflected on my three rides, I turned on my digital recorder and attempted to enter as much information as possible. Distracted, I mistakenly got onto 520 East instead of 520 West. That put me in rush hour traffic and it would now take anywhere from twenty minutes to thirty minutes to turn around. Okay, I exaggerated. But it was amazing how fifteen minutes in traffic could feel like thirty minutes.

While I was in rush hour traffic, my apologies to the creators of the defensive driving course in advance, I started to go through my email on my phone. Each day, I received a summary of my activities from Lyft. The email just arrived. I loved these daily emails.

Communication between Lyft and its drivers far surpassed communication between Uber and its drivers. Besides the faux pas of checking my email in traffic, I was feeling good. For the first time, I felt like I developed a good routine for my morning drives. Then an idea occurred to me. Joyce, struck by comments of drivers we interviewed, encouraged me to do a Friday evening drive if I wanted to get a more indepth look at the life of a driver. I felt pretty confident, maybe not tomorrow, but next week at the latest, a Friday night drive would be in my future.

LOST
December 8, 2017, Friday

Trips	Time on Road	Miles	Earnings	Vehicle Cost	Real Earnings	Hourly Wage
2	1 hr 5 min	21	$21.54	-$10.50	$11.04	$10.19

I was definitely in the holiday spirit. Dressed in a festive holiday jacket, I cranked up the holiday music and went off to pick up Eli at the Westin.

Eli

As I pulled up to the Westin, I saw Eli chatting away with the valet, as if they were best friends. Eli looked both outgoing and charismatic, I knew I was in for a good ride. And Eli, from San Francisco, did not disappoint.

Eli was headed to work, but at the end of the day, he was driving to Portland, to enjoy a weekend with some of his friends who were flying up from southern California. Eli, as if speaking to a professional, sought my advice. "I'm going to SeaTac and picking up a rental car. How long would you say it takes to get from Portland from SeaTac?"

How could such a simple question sound so endearing? I had to give a thoughtful answer. Then I realized I had what Joyce called a "man crush". No matter, I was feeling empowered.

If I blurted out the quickest answer, the answer would have been easy and most probably wrong. Pondering the question, I suddenly realized I did not have an answer. Given the fast growth in the Pacific northwest, I was no longer sure how long it would take to drive from SeaTac to Portland, so I pivoted and offered him my latest experience of driving south to Tacoma.

"A few weeks ago," I said, "I dropped off a fare at SeaTac, then not knowing the destination, picked up another fare whose destination was as far south in Tacoma as one could go. The trip took a little over an hour. So, after you leave SeaTac, you will have to go south and it will probably take you at least an hour until you have travelled through Tacoma. And because I had a passenger, I was in the car pool lane so I was able to move a lot quicker through traffic. You probably have another three hours after you get out of Tacoma."

Eli was an optimist. "Well," he said. I used to live in LA, so I'll get through it. You know, it will be nice when Tesla is able to deliver its autonomous driving vehicles."

Eli, being from San Francisco (a forty-six minute drive to Tesla's headquarters), had an intense fascination with autonomous vehicles. Eli continued, "I am pretty excited about the new Tesla glass. I've had a chance to see Tesla's Model 3. Based on the design, you get what you pay for. But," and here he emphasized but, "it comes with the new Tesla Glass, and that is what everyone wants."

I knew about the Tesla's Model 3, an affordable version (starts at 35K) of Tesla's Model S (starts at 68K) and Model X (starts at 79K). I was not aware of the Tesla glass. Eli was happy to educate me. "Basically, the entire glass wall on the dash is turned into an HD projector screen. The possibilities are endless. You can reduce heat, offer touch control, and display images. Plus, the glass roof also acts as a solar roof. It is amazing."

Fascinating, I thought. I now know that the autonomous vehicle will not only replace me, but will place me in an amusement park on four wheels.

I dropped Eli off at Nintendo America, the game company's North American headquarters. I should have guessed. The Tesla Models S will not be an amusement park, as much as a Nintendo game simulation on four wheels. Speaking with Eli was like speaking with a futurist.

I said my goodbye to Eli, marveling at his charisma. He must make friends with everyone he meets. With lots of food for thought, I decided to return to downtown Bellevue. When I got onto the highway, I was tagged for another ride. Traffic was congested and I was moving slowly when for some reason, the ride was cancelled. A minute later, another ride came in and I was headed back to the Westin.

Ozzie

I picked up Ozzie at the Westin and headed off to the Microsoft Conference Center. Ozzie, like Eli, was a young professional living in the Bay area. An engineer, Ozzie travelled around a lot. He previously lived in Singapore and LA, and he was at the tail end of two weeks of pretty heavy international travel. Unfortunately, I might have made his travels feel longer.

We arrived on the Microsoft Campus when the navigation system said we arrived at the Microsoft Conference Center. We had not arrived. Google burned me again. I was turning into a conspiracy theorist. Was Google sabotaging Microsoft?

I decided to abandon technology and travel the old-fashioned way. I followed Microsoft campus signage to finally get Ozzie to Building 33, the Microsoft Conference Center. Ozzie was frustrated and confused as the entrance was not the same as the entrance he arrived at a day earlier. I accompanied Ozzie into the Conference Center, only to find there were two different entrances to the Conference Center. We were at the right building, but at the back entrance. So, we arrived, sort of. Ozzie was frustrated and I was embarrassed.

At this point, I was the one wishing for a self-driving car. As a driver, the experience of the passenger is paramount. I was terribly frustrated at my inability to get Ozzie to his destination quickly. On the other hand, I learned, that for the first time, after my series of setbacks, I was finally comfortable with the idea of autonomous vehicles.

CHAPTER TWELVE

WEEKEND DRIVING

FRIDAY EVENING
December 9, 2017

Trips	Time on Road	Miles	Earnings	Vehicle Cost	Real Earnings	Hourly Wage
7	3 hr 39 min	102	$105.36	-$51.00	$54.36	$14.89

Although I started around 6 pm and drove only till 9 pm, I had a great sense of what to expect when driving on a weekend night. From professionals going to holiday parties, to stranded people in search of their home, to intoxicated passengers, to theft, I experienced the full spectrum of personalities I expected and hoped for on my first Friday night drive.

Sean

I picked up Sean and his lovely companion who were on their way to a holiday office party. They were headed to join friends in Duvall (about a forty-five minute drive in rush hour traffic) and then Sean and his colleagues would all drive together to the office party.

Sean, a human resource recruiter for IT professionals, recently located to San Francisco, was consulting for a company in Bellevue. "I've been living in India for the past five years, he said." "I had the good fortune of taking advantage of India's high-tech playgrounds to recruit India's best and brightest."

"You know," I said, "I heard that Amazon and Redmond were expanding to Vancouver, Canada so they could continue to recruit high tech employees from around the world and not worry about the United States stricter immigration policies. Do you know if that is true?"

"I've heard the same thing," Sean acknowledged. "But it has not impacted my recruiting so far."

"That's good to hear."

"That being said, I still have to deal with the occasional customs issues. I've also heard that immigration officers are starting to have goals that identify the number of people they reject. So, the conversation you're picking up makes sense."

As we talked about immigration issues, Sean's girlfriend, tucked quietly under his shoulder, became curious about me. At a pause in the conversation, she asked, "Why is a seemingly educated person like yourself driving?"

I didn't know how to take her question, so I decided to disclose what I was doing. I proceeded to tell them about my semi-retirement and my idea about writing a book on the Uberverse. "Quite honestly," I said, "I needed to get out of the house. Driving seemed like an adventure. And it has been nothing less than an adventure."

Sean was immensely pleased. "I have something for your book. I have a friend that uses UberPool to get dates. And he is very successful."

I heard about passengers using UberPool as a hook-up service, sometimes described as the "New Tinder", but I never encountered this type of passenger on any of my drives. From what I heard, passengers start with an innocuous question like, "Where are you headed." Given the high density of young riders in cities like Seattle and San Francisco, it made sense. Sean's friend lived in San Francisco.

I told Sean, "Well, whether dating is a perk of UberPool, or just plain creepy, I will definitely use it in my book."

Sean appeared interested to keep the conversation going, but I really had no interest in hearing about his friend, especially in mixed company. My guess was that the conversation turned creepy. I glanced into my rearview mirror and looked at his partner. Her body language was certainly one of discomfort or awkwardness. I changed topics.

A few minutes later, I dropped the couple off at their destination. I was surprised at how far south the conversation went. Maybe I am old-fashioned, but talking about friends trolling for women on car rides in front of a date seems out of line. I actually felt a sense of relief when we arrived.

I looked around and realized I had drove out into farmland. I had the terrible feeling that if experience was an indicator of future events, I would be returning through rush hour traffic, alone. I was happy to be wrong because almost immediately, I got another passenger. The question now was where would the next passenger take me, Idaho? Surprisingly, on my first weekend night drive, I would be staying close to home.

Martin

Martin was waving me down as soon as my car was within sight. A large fellow, Martin opened the front door and plopped himself in the front seat of my car. I heard this was a common practice with Lyft, but my morning passengers, the majority urban professionals, rarely sat in the front seat. Martin, laden with a backpack and an assortment of accoutrements, was doing a lot of work to squeeze himself inside the front seat.

When Martin finally shut the door, I started to slowly move out of the parking lot until I saw him shudder. Martin was not seat-belted. I brought the car to a gentle stop.

I said, "Look, I am going to pull over here. Take your time getting situated, and we can then take off. No hurries, no worries."

Martin began disassembling the various items he was carrying. Five minutes later, we were off. It looked like Martin came from a camping trip, so I asked him an indirect question, hoping to find out more on what brought him to the restaurant. "How is the Chinese food there?"

Martin had some communication challenges, speaking a little too loud, a little too fast, and a little too direct. "I did not eat there," he said. "I just got off of work and then arrived at the restaurant when I called to get a Lyft."

"Where do you work?" I asked.

"I work at Microsoft in the cafeteria. I stock biodegradable silverware and napkins and when I am not doing that, I clean counters."

I have no idea why I asked this, but it came out of my mouth all the same. "I used to stock a salad bar when I was in high school. Do you stock plates?"

"NOT PLATES," he yelled.

Okay, I thought. This guy is probably closer to the autistic side of the spectrum. I will tread lightly.

"That's a good job," I said, ignoring the elevated level of conversation, "stocking silverware, napkins and cleaning counters."

After a few moments, Martin seemed to have settled down. I was curious as to what brought him all the way to a Chinese restaurant in Duvall, so I asked another indirect question. "What time did you get off of work?"

"2 pm," Martin replied.

I looked at my app and saw that I picked up Martin at 5:47 pm. Martin walked for three hours and forty-seven minutes. I said, "You've been walking a long time."

"When I got off work, I was going to hire a Lyft and go to McCormick Park in Duvall, but I could not afford the twenty dollars. So, I decided to walk with Siri (Apple's personal intelligent assistant). Siri kept giving me bad directions on dangerous roads. So, I would turn when Siri told me to turn and start walking until Siri told me where to go next. But then I would find a street closed and have to turn and wait for Siri to tell me where to go next. Finally, Siri and I ended up at the Chinese Restaurant. I was too tired to walk anymore."

I chuckled to myself. Martin appeared to have a personal relationship with Siri. He spoke about her as if she was a real person. At first, I felt bad for Martin, walking lost for almost four hours. Then, I thought, this was probably not his first date with Siri. Really, how awesome was it that Martin used technology in a more meaningful way to explore the world?

"That is an incredible journey," I said.

"Yes, Siri takes me to a lot of places. When I finally made it to the Chinese restaurant, I turned on the Lyft app and saw that I had enough money to pay for the trip home."

We were just pulling into his apartment complex when I said, "You seem to like technology?"

Mental note to self: Do not make conversation starters at the end of a ride. I wasn't sure if Martin was speaking to himself or to me, but for the next five minutes, parked in front of Martin's apartment complex, Martin explained his idea of a digital game based on the Bible. In another setting, I could see myself spending more time with Martin, but I was "on the clock".

A couple minutes into Martin's game plan, I was alerted to another passenger. I finally said, "Your digital game sounds like a great idea. Oh, look, Martin, it appears I have another passenger to pick up."

Martin took the clue, or maybe he just took me literally, but it was only then that he started to gather his things together. Another five minutes later, he was out of the car. On reflection, I am not entirely sure if I was any more real to Martin than Siri. Then I thought, no matter, there is probably a good chance Siri will be replacing me so maybe Martin has this whole thing figured out. Regardless, I enjoyed both Martin and his story.

Kerry

I rushed out of Martin's apartment complex to get to my next fare. Fortunately, Kerry, having coffee in her parents' home, was patiently waiting for me. Like Martin, Kerry opened the front door and took the seat next to me. Kerry, a bohemian Eastern European beauty in her late twenties, made herself at home.

I have to admit, I was a little uncomfortable with the young lady sitting next to me, and after a few breaths, I realized Kerry was a smoker. Some smokers smell like an ashtray. Kerry was not one of those smokers. As Kerry did not know me from Adam, I was more bothered by Kerry sitting so close to me. Having four daughters, I made a mental note to explain to my daughters that although it is allowable for them to sit in the front seat of a rideshare vehicle, it is always safer to sit in the back.

I then thought, oh, well. Kerry is more like my older stepdaughters, so I will just treat her the same way. My wife later told me she found this to be sexist, but maybe I am just old-fashioned. As it turned out, I think I was on the right track in my consideration of creating some distance.

Kerry was friendly and chatty. I said, "So where are you going?"

"I am going back to work in Redmond."

Success! I was now headed back to Bellevue. It was the first time where I took a twenty-minute drive and was able to return with a passenger.

It was Friday night, so I asked, "Pretty late to be working on a weekend?"

"I am going to meet my boyfriend there, and we are going to drive out from there."

"Is your place of work still open on a Friday night?"

"I am a bookkeeper and a manager. I have a key, so it is okay."

Somehow, the free spirit nature of Kerry and the idea of her being a finance manager was not lining up in my head. If it was true, it made Kerry even more attractive. Near the end of the ride, Kerry said, "Can I ask you a personal question?"

Having no idea where this was headed, I said, "Sure."

"How old are you?" she asked.

Not sensitive about my age, I said, "fifty-five."

"Oh," she said, "you look thirty-five."

I felt delighted and confused at the same time. I knew I did not look thirty-five. Was she flirting with me? I was pretty sure she was young enough to be my daughter. I now had more material for a second conversation with my daughters on the dangers of talking with strangers, as well as the perils of dating older men.

We pulled up to Kerry's work place and she got out of the car. I felt a little warm and a little uneasy. That seemed way too intimate. I looked at my app and saw that Kerry cancelled the ride fifteen minutes after she got into the car. I was using Google maps so I did not see the cancellation earlier. Did I just get gamed?

As the options were girl flirting with me to cancel a fare or girl flirting with me because I look younger than I appeared, I concluded that I had to have been scammed. But was it even possible to end a ride like this and not pay for it? I pulled over and went online to get the answer.

Harry, the owner and writer of the rideshare blog, described my worse fear. In one post, he acknowledged that some passengers purposefully cancel a trip during a ride in order not to pay for the ride:

> "I've never personally experienced this but I've talked to many drivers who have had passengers cancel the trip halfway through or even as soon as the ride begins. If drivers aren't looking at their phone, then they might not even know that this has happened until they get to the destination.
>
> **How To Avoid:** I always use the GPS on my phone to navigate even if I am pretty sure where we're going. That also means that I'll see a cancellation notification/text every time I glance at the phone. Just make sure that you don't do it while you're driving."[28]

This must be what other drivers mean when they talk about the risks of driving weekend nights. I had been driving professionals during the day, so, now that I was working a weekend night, did I end up with a con artist? What was I to do next? If I complained, could Kerry falsely accuse me of harassment? It would be her word against mine and I would just look like the creepy old guy. It became painfully clear to me why some drivers have a cam in their car – for situations like this one.

I shouldn't have worried, but I guess that is what happens when a young girl compliments you. I later discovered that what was cancelled was another passenger that was placed on my queue. Kerry was legit

---

[28] https://therideshareguy.com/top-10-ways-that-uber-and-lyft-passengers-are-gaming-the-system-and-how-to-prevent-it/

and I overreacted. Maybe I just had to accept the fact that a younger woman might have found me attractive. Well, I mused to myself, I am going to forget the first two conversations I was going to have with my daughters. Instead, I will tell them they can never use rideshare.

Eugene, Rob, and Eli's Party

My next three rides happened in rapid succession. I picked up Eugene at the Bravern in Bellevue and found myself driving across the lake to Seattle. Eugene worked silently the entire time.

I was now on a roll and picked up Rob and his girlfriend, enjoying their romantic banter. It was like listening to mini intellectuals discussing every subject from aesthetics to Donald Trump. It was obvious that the lovebirds were trying to impress each other, but at the very least, they impressed me.

Once I dropped them off at a trendy-looking restaurant, I picked up Eli, who along with her three friends, all in the early twenties, were headed to Bothell for a party. I would actually be making my way back home once more.

When I dropped the happy group of partygoers off, they wished me well. To my surprise, they asked me to drive safe. I was touched by their courtesy on exiting the car. I was enjoying the weekend night driving experience and decided to accept one last fare, also in Bothell.

Rita

I was approaching a neighborhood that was a little rough around the edges. I looked at the app and saw my pick-up was at the Back Door Pub, "a place for pool sharks (who play free on Sundays) and sketchy-types."[29] That did not sound good. I thought, I should have stopped when I had the chance.

I found a space right in front of the pub, parked, and looked up into what appeared to be an exceedingly seedy establishment. I had five minutes to wait, so I got out of the car to stretch my legs. I looked

---

[29] https://www.thestranger.com/locations/993332/back-door-pub

around at my surroundings, dreading what was about to walk or stagger out of the pub.

After a couple of minutes, I thought I better be prepared, so I went to the back of my car, opened my trunk, and got a shopping bag which would have to make do as a "barf bag." Just as I placed the shopping bag in the front seat of my car, a middle age couple walked out of the bar, each carrying a suitcase. The couple was smiling and waving at me.

What could I do? A little shocked at this unexpected turn of events, I smiled and waved back. I then walked to the back of my car, popped open the trunk, and stored their luggage. Rita was laughing and giggling. They did not leave the bar thirsty.

Rita was not shy and immediately laid out the series of events that led them to me. Rita and her husband just returned from Houston and instead of going home, they decided to go to their local bar where Rita's mom worked. Rita said, "It is charitable endeavor, a way to support the community." The couple definitely had a few.

Rita and her husband are the kind of people you hope to meet in a bar. They are those local barflies you find in your neighborhood bar, knowledgeable about the area and the people, and they were a hoot. I would not have been surprised if they had a few drinks on the plane before they got to the bar.

Rita's husband said to me in good-natured way, "Rita was flirting with a guy at the bar, so it was time to leave." Rita ignored her husband with a laugh. Rita then began to point out to me every bar on the way to their home.

Rita was intimately familiar with each local establishment. "This bar has drugs... We no longer go there. This one has too much drama... We're no longer welcomed there."

I dropped the happy couple off at 9 pm. They were still chatting and laughing all the way to their front door. Drunk? I don't know. Happy? Definitely.

The night was still young. But as I reflected on my night, I decided to return home. I had a good glimpse at the risks and the fun one runs into while driving on a Friday night. What would it be like driving from

9 pm to 1 am on a Friday night? I thought. I didn't know, and given how much material I already collected, I was calling it a night.

I had one more week of driving before I would leave to spend three weeks in New York for the holidays. Over the holidays, I would take time to edit my entries. And just maybe, I would have enough of a glimpse into the Uberverse to publish a book.

CHRISTMAS SPIRIT
December 11, 2017, Monday

Trips	Time on Road	Miles	Earnings	Vehicle Cost	Real Earnings	Hourly Wage
3	1 hr 30 min	28	$23.62	-$14.00	$9.62	$6.41

I turned on Lyft and after ten minutes of silence, pulled over and parked in front of the Rite Aid next to my building. Not one passenger and it was already 8:30 am, so I turned on Uber. And in what became an increasing pattern, within a couple of minutes, I got tagged by an Uber passenger. All three fares would be Uber.

On the bright side, once again, I was back to driving working professionals, one local, one out of state, and one out of country, to their work place – a far different crowd from my Friday night experience. I was a little relieved to leave the weekend of unexpected rides to the reliability of my passengers on the eastside.

Linda

Linda, from Miami, FL, stepped into my car and said, "Oh, I LOVE Christmas music!"

I took an instant liking to Linda. Sirius had a channel that played twenty-four hours of holiday songs. I played the channel all December and Linda was the second passenger to compliment the music.

Linda asked me in a hopeful voice, "Do you think we will see some snow?"

"I'm afraid," I said, knowing I would be the bearer of bad news, "that the chances are not good. I am leaving to go to New York on Thursday for the holidays and I am pretty sure I will see snow."

"I envy you. I'm from Miami and we never get snow."

"That is a coincidence. I just came back from Orlando a couple of weeks ago. I envy you. The weather is beautiful."

"Disney World or Universal Studios?" Linda asked.

"Disney World," I said to sounds of laugher. "I'm pretty sure it is cheaper to travel to Germany and take in some real castles than to buy a four-day pass at Disney World."

"Oh, yes," she agreed. "When Hurricane Irma came, we evacuated to the resorts in Orlando because they have better back-up systems. What was supposed to be a disaster relief experience turned into a two-grand vacation experience even though the parks were closed. I even bought a Harry Potter sweatshirt as I had nothing to do but shop at the hundreds of gift stores that remained open."

It didn't take us long to get to TMobile, Linda's destination. We were both still carrying on and laughing. I wanted to thank Linda for being such a great start to my day, but I knew it wouldn't be professional. At the very least, hopefully, for passengers like Linda, the experience was reciprocal.

Still not giving up on Lyft, I switched the Lyft app on and the Uber app on. Uber responded immediately.

Bhagyashri

I picked up Bhagyashri at an apartment complex near Bellevue College. I first thought she was a college student. As soon as she got into the car, Bhagyashri called her father and proceeded to talk to him almost the entire way. Once again, I guessed wrong as she was on her way to work.

As we got closer to Bhagyashri's work place, we entered the darkest fog I ever experienced in my life. Even though she was on the phone, I said, "Look. Have you ever seen fog like this? I can barely see what is in front of me."

Bhagyashri got off her phone call and stared out the front window. "Yes, it is bad." She then pointed forward and said: "My building is over there."

I saw nothing but a thick wall of fog. It was eerily creepy. Then, out of nowhere, appeared a large eight story building. We were both stunned. Then, for no reason whatsoever, we both started laughing.

It was a short trip but it was worth it just for the experience of driving into such dense fog. I dropped off Bhagyashri, and like before, switched on both rideshare apps, hoping Lyft would not disappoint yet again. And for the final time, Uber responded and I turned off the Lyft app for the day.

Gunner

I glanced down at my earnings and had a hunch my hourly rate for the day would be low. I found out later I was correct. I already saw two large gaps in my trips that day. The first gap had to do with attempting to use Lyft exclusively. I spent too much time waiting for Lyft to present me with a passenger. The second gap had to do with picking up passengers. When I left to get my final passenger, Gunner, I had to get on 90, then get off 90. It took me nine minutes and I probably travelled five miles. That also cost me.

Fortunately, Gunner and his associate, both men from Sweden, more than made up for the loss. I reversed my role as Uber driver and became tourist guide. Both men asked a lot of questions about the area, so I gave them a short course on the demographics, weather patterns, and business opportunities of the Seattle area. They were excited to be here and there really is nothing better than basking in the energy of an appreciative audience.

Gunner told me that when they arrived at the airport, they noticed there were several ride companies available. They were not sure what to make of it, but they liked all of the choices. By the time we reached the Microsoft Campus, we moved from local demographics, to rideshare, to the implications of autonomous vehicle in various accident scenarios.

We concluded that in an accident, an autonomous vehicle was more likely to use data to protect its passengers first. This put the other driver and even bystanders that might be innocently standing nearby at risk. I'm sure if Gunner and his colleague were in the car another five minutes, we would have moved into a completely different direction. But the two men had jobs to do and I was on my way home.

CHAPTER THIRTEEN

REGRET

MELANCHOLY
December 12, 2017, Tuesday

Trips	Time on Road	Miles	Earnings	Vehicle Cost	Real Earnings	Hourly Wage
3	1 hr 35 min	26	$25.19	-$13.00	$12.19	$7.70

It was my second to last day of driving before I headed out to New York and quite possibly my second to last day of my driving career. I knew I loved this job when I said to myself, I wish I could drive while I am in New York.

I was feeling a little melancholy, knowing tomorrow could very well be my last. I now had enough content to complete a book. But as I waited for a Lyft call, again, in the parking lot at Rite Aid, a thought occurred to me. Maybe, just maybe, my journey was not quite over. The possibility of a sequel entered into my head. What about a series of night-time rides over six or seven weekends? I would give it some thought. I would need to pick up a car cam and most probably have an uncomfortable conversation with Joyce on the added risk of night drives, but I began to feel inspired once again, or maybe just hopeful that something I enjoyed so much might continue. I obviously did not want the driving to end and used another book as an excuse to continue. No doubt about it, I was sucked in.

Unfortunately, so close to my final day, I hit a record low in earnings. The wage culprits:
1. Long drives to pick up passengers, and;
2. My first ever bathroom break.

Since I never worked an eight-hour shift, I never took a break. On this particular day, nature called and the consequence of stopping severely impacted my hourly wage. I thought about removing my break time of fifteen minutes out of my spreadsheet, but didn't drivers deserve a break?

Jesse

I picked up Jesse at the Bellevue Transit Center. He took a bus from Seattle and was now completing his journey to work via Lyft. So many people seemed to be giving up their cars for public transportation. At the same time, it seemed like they were spending more money to get to and from the workplace. Maybe their time was worth the investment as they were freed up to work while I drove.

Jesse did just that. He entered the car and was on his phone immediately, doing work. Yes, he could have been playing games. But I gave him the benefit of the doubt. The ride was short and I dropped Jesse off at his office building.

I turned on both Lyft and Uber and something unexpected happened. I was hailed by Uber, followed by a hail from Lyft. I chose not to accept the Uber trip and for a second time in a row, picked up a Lyft passenger. Maybe I should have taken the Uber passenger?

Billy

I arrived at Billy's apartment building and found myself in a quandary. Billy was not outside, there was no parking, the intersection was under construction, and it was rush hour. I had to leave and make a loop around his block, driving another five minutes to get back to the apartment. When I arrived a second time, Billy was still nowhere to be found. I saw a place I could double-park across from the construction zone. Unfortunately, there were two police officers walking the construction site. I double-parked, directly across the street from the police officers, and called Billy. I informed him of my location and let him know I was adjacent to two police officers. Several minutes later with no signs of Billy, I called again and Billy said he was on his way.

After what seemed like forever under the watchful eyes of the police officers, Billy, wearing a Seahawks ball cap, finally arrived. Like Jesse, he was immediately on his phone. Unlike Jesse, he appeared agitated, in this case, he was constantly squirming in the back seat. My prejudices kicked in. I thought, drug addict? His nervous energy rubbed off on me. I felt nervous.

Billy's destination was the Seattle Seahawks corporate headquarters in Renton. I made fairly good time as I hoped to have him out of my car as soon as possible. When we arrived, the complex had not yet opened and the gate was locked. Billy asked me to pull over adjacent to the security fence to let him off. He got out of the car and he then proceeded to walk around the chain link fence well past the entrance. I had no idea where he was going.

I needed to use the restroom and spotted a McDonald's so I made my hurried escape. Driving over the I-405 bypass to get to the restaurant, a homeless man, dressed in Seahawks garb, looked at me, beat his chest, and yelled to me, "Go, Seahawks." Hmm, I thought. This is starting to feel a lot like Friday night.

Once out of McDonalds, I turned the Lyft app on and started back toward downtown Bellevue. I was in heavy traffic, once again wondering how the delay in traffic and the mileage driven would impact my hourly wage, when I got another Lyft call to pick up Kevin in Factoria.

Kevin

Kevin sent me a couple of texts providing more specific directions to his location. It was difficult to check text messages, drive and speak into a digital recorder. But at the very least, unlike my drive to pick up Jesse, I had a heads up that the location would not be easy to navigate.

I was driving through a sea of apartment buildings via multiple parking lots when I was abruptly blocked by four concrete pylons. I turned around, drove back out to a main street and finally came to a main road. I checked Kevin's text and travelled a little bit farther to the location Kevin identified in his text message, Building Six. Thank you, Kevin.

Kevin, an employee at TMobile, was running late to work. He told me: "My one-year old daughter is sick so I am helping my wife, a stay-at-home mom, to care for her."

"That is such a huge responsibility," I said, "a one-year old daughter."

Kevin was immensely proud of his baby girl. "Sometimes," he said, grinning ear to ear, "my daughter sleeps in our bedroom. She gets up at 5 a.m., I take her into our bed, and she will start talking and cooing in my ear."

Having four daughters, I nostalgically remembered such times. Kevin, like me, enjoyed talking about himself and his family. And Kevin, I found, was a man of the world. He was born and raised in southern India and had been in the United State for three years. Just before emigrating to the United States, Kevin received his graduate degree in England. I could tell he missed England.

"Why did you decide to move to the United States from England?" I asked.

"In England, a lot of careers stall at the mid-management level," he answered. "America has a lot more opportunities and is more tolerant."

"I'm glad to hear that," I said.

"But I would love to have a job teaching at a university in England. You know, you should think about travelling to southern India. You would enjoy it."

I wholeheartedly agreed. "India has been on my bucket list. It is just such a large country and I wouldn't even know where to begin to travel."

Kevin proceeded to give me recommendations. I instantly liked Kevin. He had pride of place, managed a successful career, and was a proud and committed father. After my first couple of drives and a homeless person on a bridge, Kevin was a breath of fresh air. I even thought about inviting his family to dinner. But again, Lyft driver.

I couldn't help but think that the world of rideshare opened so many doors to me. On any trip, I never knew what to expect. Passengers reflected all people and touched all parts of the world. Sure, driving could be overwhelming. But as I said before, you never knew what present you would be opening next, and, regretfully, you couldn't take home any of the gifts.

CHRISTMAS CHEER
December 12, 2017, Thursday

Trips	Time on Road	Miles	Earnings	Vehicle Cost	Real Earnings	Hourly Wage
2	1 hr 31 min	57	$63.40	-$28.50	$34.90	$23.01

I felt sad as today was potentially my last day as a driver, so I turned on Sirius to the holiday station, in the hopes of some Christmas cheer. I pulled over at the Rite Aid next to my building and was listening to *The Christmas Song* by Nat King Cole, when I was hailed by Jesslyn.

Jesslyn

I pulled up to Jesslyn's apartment building and saw two police officers walking around their patrol car. I was not sure about Jesslyn's exact location, so I pulled up behind the police car and immediately dialed Jesslyn's number. Jesslyn picked up immediately.

"Hello," she said. "We are just in front of the police car."

I pulled around the police car and saw Jesslyn, an older woman, Jesslyn's mother, and a young man, Jesslyn's husband, all carrying suitcases. I said to them, looking over at the police officers, "Well, this is quite the welcome."

They laughed nervously. Okay, I thought. A little anxiety here. I proceeded to load their suitcases in the car. As the young man sat down in the front seat, Jessyln and her mother sat in the back. Jesslyn and her mom were speaking Russian to each other. I heard Jesslyn's mom say in English, "Alaska Airlines", so I immediately knew the destination and settled in for the quietest ride of my short career.

The quiet in my car was deafening and I was suffocating from the silence. The family was eerily quiet, not a word. Nada. Maybe limited English?

I was just getting off 405 and approaching the airport when the young man said in a heavy Russian accent, "Christmas songs. I love them."

After a moment of shock, I said, "Yes, the songs are peaceful and given rush hour traffic, the music has a calming effect."

"Yes," he agreed. "And the songs are all old."

"I love the classics," I said, to which he nodded vigorously as we approached the terminal. "Here we are," I continued, "Alaska Airlines, which I believe is your departure gate."

I pulled up and parked behind another police car and pointed directly at the patrol car. "Look, police to greet us and police to send us off."

I was glad when they started to laugh, this time not nervously, but relaxed. Feeling good at our brief exchange, I jumped out of the car and retrieved their suitcases. To my surprise, the young man raised his hand to shake my hand. I took his hand in mine and said, "Happy holidays!"

I was feeling good at the change of events when I was immediately hailed by another fare. This was going to be a great final day. I accepted the ride without looking at the pick-up point. As I followed the GPS voice guidance to the destination, I was not aware I was headed to the Lyft and Uber pick-up point at the airport.

When I finally looked down to identify the location of the pickup point, I thought, Damn! My car isn't allowed to pick up people at the airport. The only cars allowed at the pick up point are fuel efficient vehicles (mostly hybrid or electric) or specially designated vehicles like Uber Black. My car did not qualify.

What to do? Oh, well, as I accepted the call, I had to follow through and pick up the passenger. So, if airport security fined me one hundred dollars, I would just pay the fine.

I pulled into the parking lot, got a parking ticket, and approached a fork in the road. If I went left, I would enter the public parking garage. If I went right, I would be following a taxi about to drive under an overhead sign that read "Authorized Vehicles Only". If I was going to follow through on my misadventure, I would have to take the lane for authorized vehicles to reach the drop zone. I did not take the lane for authorized vehicles as I knew my car was not authorized, and missed the entrance to the drop zone.

I decided to leave the parking garage in the hope I could find another way into the drop zone. Driving out of the parking garage, I pulled up to the booth at the exit gate. I put the parking ticket up to the scanner and was relieved to find there was no charge.

I made another lap around the parking lot, thinking there might be another entrance from the street outside the terminal. There was no other entrance, so I drove back into the parking lot, and retrieved another parking ticket. This time, I double parked outside the drop zone, got out of the car, ran into the drop zone and flagged down Hamilton.

Hamilton

Hamilton must have been waiting for me for ten minutes so he was not jumping for joy on meeting me. I said, "Please follow me as I am parked just adjacent to the drop zone. I apologize for being late, but vehicles in the drop zone are required to have gas mileage of forty-five miles per gallon or more. Mine does not. I am not sure why I was called on this fare, but I will clarify later with Lyft."

Hamilton did not care, he was in a hurry, "Well, as long as you can get me to my meeting by 10."

Feeling guilty, I said, "Listen, if I can't get you to your meeting, I will reimburse your fare." I could tell from Hamilton's body language that my offer did not sit well. He had a meeting to get to. He did not care about the money, only the inconvenience.

So, I followed up with, "Well, your meeting is much more important so I will do everything in my power to get you there."

When I arrived at the parking exit, I realized I misplaced my parking ticket. Aghhhhhh!!!! When I pushed the help button, a cranky voice told me to pull back out, a dangerous maneuver, and move to the cash exit lane. I did as I was told, made the dangerous exit, drove up to the attendant, and informed her of my lost parking ticket. Fortunately, Hamilton was busy on the phone.

The gate keeper said I would have to pay a full one day fare, thirty dollars. I did not want to cause a fuss as I was trying to make up for lost time. I handed over thirty dollars. If Hamilton thought anything of my out of pocket expenditure, he said nothing. But then again, he was on a conference call, discussing a thirteen million dollar to sixteen-million-dollar acquisition of what sounded like an IP license.

My mistake, my loss, but my priorities were still in order. I needed to move and get the passenger to his meeting on time. I would drive safe, but I would drive smart, so I kept my attention focused on the road. When I picked up my phone to get a better look at traffic, I felt a piece of paper sticking to the back of my phone. I pulled the piece of paper off my phone and looked at it. It was the airport parking ticket. I stuck it to the back of my phone so I wouldn't forget it. I almost laughed.

Forty minutes later and another apology, I got Hamilton to his destination, ten minutes ahead of schedule. He got out of his car, thanked me, and made a beeline for his meeting. What a stressful way to end the day.

It might have been only two rides, but it was quite the roller coaster. Plus, my last ride resembled in many ways my very first ride, so there was some poetic justice. I made mistakes, but regardless of the cost, I maintained my commitment to service

I looked at my earnings and saw that my first fare tipped me a very generous five dollars. Hamilton, as I expected, left nothing. The next day, I would discover that Hamilton actually left me a ten-dollar tip. That's another thing I came to love about driving; people continued to surprise me in positive ways.

As I headed home, I decided, like I told Hamilton, to get in contact with Lyft. I waited on the phone six and a half minutes. The man who answered the phone was very friendly. But there was nothing he could do. The bottom line was that Lyft would continue to offer rides to a restricted area even though my vehicle was not authorized to take such rides. Hmmmm.

Lyft and Uber identify themselves as tech companies. I thought, how can a company like Lyft have the technology to introduce self-driving vehicles, but cannot write code so that drivers are not invited to locations where their vehicle is not authorized? I was frustrated. Even their automated phone system got on my nerves. Thirty dollars out of pocket will do that to you.

If I was honest with myself, some of my frustration was a result of my not wanting this job to end. The job was a roller coaster, but I loved it. What other opportunity put me in front of so many different people? What other job allowed me to get a real sense of the breadth and depth of the community I lived in? And in spite of some of the hurdles and the low pay, I found I would happily recommend the experience, just not full-time.

Tomorrow, I would leave for New York. I still had the opportunity to interview a driver on the way to SeaTac and another driver when I got to Newark. But after that, I would do some editing, write a final chapter, and publish my book. I could feel I was near the end of my rideshare journey. And that feeling felt a lot like loss, the loss of walking away from a good friend.

CHAPTER FOURTEEN

MY HERO

ROLE MODEL
December 14, 2017, Thursday

On my way to Newark, I and my two youngest daughters (Joyce was flying separately due to a work commitment) would take two Lyft rides, one to get to the Seattle airport and one to get to my in-laws from the Newark airport. For interview purposes, it did not work as planned. My driver to the airport spoke very little English, so I just sat back and enjoyed the ride. Fortunately, my ride from the Newark airport to my in-law's home was a much different story. I met my hero.

Carlos

Carlos, a sort of Latino Robert Redford, picked us up in his impeccably clean, brand new, black GMC Yukon. Stepping into the car, I made myself comfortable on the spacious, black leather seats. I noticed two phones on the dash, one for Uber and one for Lyft.

Carlos had a heavy Spanish accent, so I asked, "Where are you from originally?"

"Peru," he said.

"Beautiful country," I said. "I love Peru."

"Oh, you have been to Peru?"

"Yes. I spent a couple of weeks taking college students from Cusco to Machu Picchu. Very beautiful. How often do you go back to Peru?"

"Not very often. I've been living here for 25 years. My whole family came over in 1975. First was my aunt, then my grandfather and grandmother. Everyone is now here."

Carlos's family had three generations of family now living in the United States. Over the last two decades, the family members assimilated into the American melting pot. Carlos talked about annual family gatherings at Christmas, his son who was going to attend University of Pennsylvania in the fall. Carlos was very proud of his family.

"What did you do before you became a driver?" I asked.

"I've been doing this for a year and a half. Before, I was a truck driver."

"So, there was probably very little transition from driving a truck to driving for Uber and Lyft. I imagine driving a truck is not easy, especially when you drive long distances. It must be hard on the body. Why did you decide to make the change?"

"Yes, you are right. Driving a truck was tough on the body. When I was driving the truck, I was also never home. That's a problem. Now, I drive private, Lyft, Uber and Juno. I have more time to be at home."

"What's Juno?"

"It's a new rideshare company. It's been here for two years, and it only works in New York City."

"Is the pay any better on Juno?"

"Juno takes a smaller cut off every ride, just ten percent compared to Uber's twenty to twenty-five percent."

Unbeknownst to me, Juno launched its ride sharing services in New York City in 2016. It had high hopes of creating a business model that ultimately would benefit drivers. Juno was setting up an equity structure that would allow its drivers a fifty percent stake in its founder's equity by 2026. But in 2017, the program was discontinued when Juno was acquired by Gett. The merger eliminated the driver equity program, ending a promising partnership between drivers and the company, and left both passengers and drivers confused as to Gett's intentions.

I was also intrigued when Carlos said he drove independently. I asked, "What do you mean by private?"

"I have my own customers. They like my car, especially when they have a big family. They call me and I'm there. I also have three different companies that depend on me for driving."

I was impressed. Carlos was the first person I met that did rideshare and private drives. "That is pretty incredible," I said. "You appear to be maximizing driving at every level. And I have no doubt with your long history in transportation, you are the consummate professional. How much of your time is spent on private rides and how much of your time is spent on rideshare rides?"

"I do one or two private rides a day and the rest on Juno, Uber, or Lyft."

"Are some days better than others?"

"Oh, yes. Friday nights are my best days."

Every Friday night, Carlos worked between a fourteen-hour and sixteen-hour shift. He started around nine or ten on Friday morning and finished the next day at eight in the morning. Carlos said, "It's only one day a week, but on a good Friday, I can make between eight-hundred dollars and a thousand dollars."

"That's a pretty long day."

"My wife hates it, but it is a lot of money. When I make my amount, and if I feel tired, I turn it off and go home."

"Isn't it kind of risky, Friday nights, with people drinking, etc.?"

"It depends on the car. I do black, so I see a different type of customer. If you do XL or plus, it is certainly a different customer. So, my clientele is very different which is very nice. And… I get a higher premium for my car."

"Do you drive mostly in the city?"

"I stay mostly in New York City. I make three to four trips to the airport, two to three private trips, and the rest of the trips using Lyft, Uber and Juno."

"How many miles do you put on the car on a night like that?

"Hmmm. I put anywhere from 150 miles to 175 miles on my car."

"That's a lot of travel. Are there places you will not drive to?"

"Some drivers say they like to stay in the city. I will go all over."

"Which trips pay better, longer trips or shorter trips?"

"Longer trips are the better paid trips."

"Do you find a lot of business at the airport?"

"There are too many drivers at the airport which is why it is taking longer to get a request. There are times when I don't get any requests. I was waiting forty minutes before I got your request. I thought, ten more minutes and I will head back to New York. It is a long time to wait and not have a passenger."

"My in-laws are a little distance from New York City. Are you afraid that your next trip might pull you even farther away?"

"The app will usually keep me closer to New York. If you are a New Jersey driver, you might end up getting sent farther into New Jersey. I live in New Jersey, but my plates are from New York. When I drop you off, hopefully, someone will call and if not, I will keep going on my way to New York. It is like fifty percent I will get a request. I have New York plates, that is why they want me to be in New York."

As we pulled up to my mother-in-law's house, I thought, most of the premium car drivers are driving full time. They are also a lot more polished. People like Carlos, and they are the rare few, certainly seem to be making a living at this work. Carlos was definitely the driver I wanted to grow up to be.

Could Carlos really be making eight-hundred dollars to a thousand dollars on a Friday night? When I plugged in the numbers to my spreadsheet, based on the numbers Carlos provided, his hourly rate turned out to be fifty-one dollars and eighty-eight cents per hour. I was starting to have a change of heart. Who knows? With a premium car, and in the right locale, and an incredible work ethic, maybe one could sustain a full-time livable wage.

And it wasn't only Carlos that was driving in the family. Carlos' wife, a nursing assistant, was even in on the action. On the way to work, about fifteen minutes away, Carlos' wife would leave a little early, turn on the app, and take a passenger. As Carlos said, "At least it pays for the gas."

Carlos pulled into my in-law's driveway, got out of the car, and took out our bags. He shook my hand and wished me a Merry Christmas. After meeting Carlos, I was feeling merry indeed.

Conclusion

WHAT A RIDE!

"I must go down to the sea again, to the lonely sea and the sky; and all I ask is a tall ship and a star to steer her by."[30]

John Masefield

No reason to drive any longer as I worked on a few finishing touches of my book on the Uberverse. But I couldn't help myself. Every time I stepped into my car, I got excited, thinking about incredible adventures. I started to feel all of the old longings. What new destination? Who would I meet? Would we bond?

The kids were at school and Joyce was working so I made my way down to the parking garage. I stepped into the car, seatbelted myself in, and turned on the app. I was excited, no longer bound by my writing or shackled by spread sheets or concerns about minimum hourly rates. I was ready to sail into new and unchartered waters.

A passenger beckoned and I was once again piloting my ship to a destination unknown. Rain pounded on my car, I ventured into Seattle's stormy sea. Sure, there were risks, pirates in the form of aggressive drivers, but it certainly added to the excitement, if not the challenge.

I made two trips. I bonded. I once again found my sealegs. Time to close the final chapter of this book.

---

[30] https://www.brainyquote.com/quotes/john_masefield_389919

LEARN ABOUT THE WORLD

> *Sweet dreams are made of this*
> *Who am I to disagree?*
> *I travel the world and the seven seas*
> *Everybody's looking for something.*[31]
>
> Eurythmics

I loved driving. Each passenger was an adventure. Every trip was another opportunity to get to know the community.

Maybe I didn't get to travel the seven seas. But how else would I have discovered T-Mobile in Factoria, Facebook in Seattle, and the Wildwoods Distillery in Bothell? One day, I was lost in a vast stretch of farmland. Another day, I was struggling to navigate an obstacle course through Seattle's urban jungle. The horizons were endless.

There were good neighborhoods and there were bad neighborhoods. Good neighborhoods could be romantic. Bad neighborhoods could be dangerous, or just downright depressing. But like seafarers of old, I was open to where the winds took me, and the winds did not disappoint.

Every destination was like a new port. When I make land, people from all over the world stepped into my car. Most wanted to talk and it didn't take a lot to get them going. And at least for a few moments, I was their greatest fan, taking in their insights, perspectives, loves, and even hates.

Driving was not only a great escape, driving was the great American equalizer. Anyone can drive. One did not have to be wealthy to drive. One no longer needs a sailboat to explore the world. A canoe (Ford Focus), or a yacht (Lincoln SUV), would suffice and there were multiple other vehicles to fit anyone's budgetary requirements.

There was a dark side. Just like sailors who had to worry about scurvy, drivers faced their own challenges, most notably from a faceless

---

[31] http://www.metrolyrics.com/sweet-dreams-are-made-of-this-lyrics-eurythmics.html

boss, a shipwreck in the making. Declining earnings, lack of training, poor to non-existent benefits, some drivers were no better off than indentured servants. The car was leased to a company, there were no benefits, and the faceless boss just didn't care.

Faceless Boss

> Let's recap: Uber CEO Travis Kalanick joins President Trump's business council, and faces an immediate backlash; Uber is accused of undermining a taxi driver protest at JFK airport; the #DeleteUber hashtag goes viral; Susan Fowler speaks her mind; Waymo files its lawsuit; a self-driving Uber runs a red light; a self-driving Uber crashes; Travis Kalanick is caught on camera being a jerk; we learn about Uber executives visiting a South Korean escort bar; Apple threatens to remove Uber from the App Store; "Greyball;" "Hell;" Anthony Levandowski pleads the Fifth; Anthony Levandowski is fired; Uber considers smearing a rape victim in India; many Uber executives resign; Kalanick resigns; Lyft outpaces Uber; London bans Uber; the new CEO apologizes; a failed auto-leasing program is canceled; a major Uber investor sues Kalanick, who countersues; Uber is subject to five separate criminal investigations; Uber is fined for enabling unqualified drivers; a data hack exposes personal information of 57 million riders and drivers; the hacker is paid off and the hack is covered up; and (last but not least) Uber's secret spying unit is exposed, and it sounds insane.
>
> *The Verge*, December 29, 2017[32]

Uber's growth has been phenomenal, extending its reach all over the world, yet not only did Uber bleed 3.2 billion dollars in losses for 2017, Uber embarked on a series of mind-blowing and seemingly endless scandals. Yet, rideshare providers like Uber have changed the world.

---

[32] https://www.theverge.com/2017/12/29/16820474/2017-tech-recap-uber-scandal-waymo-lawsuits-travis-kalanick

In the entire Uberverse, can you remember the last time you saw a hitchhiker? Uber reported 2 million drivers globally, what could be looked upon as a mega city.³³ And for people like myself, working on a part-time basis, the number of drivers were even larger. Lyft alone had 700,000 drivers nationwide, so the real number of drivers was significantly higher.³⁴ It truly is a world unto itself.

The drivers I met were travel warriors, especially those that worked full-time. Yet, because drivers "work for themselves", a convenient selling point for companies who then invest little to nothing in its drivers, little consideration or study was paid to the experience or financial well-being of the driver.

When MIT released a deeply flawed study, it came with considerable controversy. Everyone appeared to be debating just how much a driver actually makes, including the drivers. Most drivers, I am sad to say, are deluded when it comes to their real earnings. They certainly don't make as much as they think, and in my conversations with various drivers, they rarely factored in all of the costs.

Multiple factors are squeezing driver earnings. More drivers, less work, more crowded streets, increased regulations, companies constantly squeezing drivers to make up for their losses, tax consequences, gas prices, vehicle wear and tear, and greater wait times. The tragedy is that the list does not stop there. No health insurance, no life insurance, no dental insurance, no eye insurance, no sick leave, the road ahead for drivers is fraught with dangers. At least according to my spreadsheet and my interviews with drivers, the job, as a sole source income, is unsustainable.

So, yes, tips matter. Drivers were completely dependent on the generosity of passengers. But in one of Uber's biggest marketing ploys, passengers have been trained not to tip, and the fiscal woes of the driver continued unabated. Drivers once again were placed in the roughest part of the sea.

---

[33] http://money.cnn.com/2017/12/18/technology/uber-drivers-180-days-of-change/index.html

[34] https://www.bizjournals.com/baltimore/news/2017/12/11/lyft-drivers-can-earn-discounted-degrees-thanks-to.html

Finally, whether it be Uber, Lyft or some other rideshare service, companies suffer from a serious lack of controls. Drivers were provided little to no oversight, training, or any meaningful evaluation and follow-up. There was no discernible dress code and the standards for the cleanliness of a vehicle were nonexistent. Were companies biding time until they perfected their autonomous vehicles?

I told many passengers I felt like a 19th century horse and buggy driver waiting for the introduction of the automobile. The automobile took twenty to thirty years until it finally replaced the buggy. The same fate awaits present day drivers who, like the dinosaur and the buggy, will become extinct. Will it take ten years, twenty years, thirty years, I do not know. But it is certainly inevitable and certainly something I have seriously reflected upon with my family, my friends, other drivers, and my passengers.

Conclusion: End of an Era

My driving experience was everything I dreamed, and more. I feel deeply for the hundreds of thousands of drivers that depend on rideshare for employment. I have the deepest respect for the many passengers who rely on its convenience.

I confess, my perspective is limited. Older than most drivers, I do not rely on driving for my income. I drove part time and experienced minimal back pain. I cannot imagine the pain experienced by drivers working eight to ten hour days regularly. Weather patterns are totally mental (Noah's Ark comes to mind), and the area I drove was ridiculously expensive. But I imagine, it is the uniqueness of each part of this country that offers value to this particular line of work. Given all these limitations, I hope, at the very least, I provided a glimpse into the world of rideshare.

Driving is the easiest job I ever applied for. No boss watched over me. I set my own hours. I met and dialogued with people of every ilk. I visited areas of the Pacific northwest I never saw before.

Who knows? If you are in the Seattle area and you request an Uber or a Lyft, you might get me. It is a hard habit to break. But wherever you go, if you call for an Uber, a Lyft, or your rideshare company of choice, please, on behalf of my fellow drivers, tip, and if you can, tip generously.

The End

www.ingramcontent.com/pod-product-compliance
Lightning Source LLC
Chambersburg PA
CBHW052254220526
45471CB00001B/329